THE STRUGGLE BETWEEN ENGLAND AND FRANCE FOR SUPREMACY IN INDIA

THE

STRUGGLE BETWEEN ENGLAND AND FRANCE

FOR

SUPREMACY IN INDIA

(THE "LE BAS" PRIZE ESSAY FOR 1886)

BY

EDWARD J. RAPSON

GYAN

Published by

GYAN

Gyan Publishing House
5, Ansari Road
Daryaganj, New Delhi-110002
Phone: 011-47034999, 9811692060
E-mail: books@gyanbooks.com

Distribution Network
gyanbooks.com
India, USA, Canada, UK, Australia

ISBN: 978-93-6433-053-4 (PB)
First Published, 1887

2nd Impression 2024

Printed at: Gyan Press, Delhi.

THE STRUGGLE BETWEEN ENGLAND AND FRANCE FOR SUPREMACY IN INDIA

Author: EDWARD J. RAPSON

THE
STRUGGLE BETWEEN ENGLAND AND FRANCE
FOR SUPREMACY IN INDIA.

THE STRUGGLE BETWEEN ENGLAND AND FRANCE FOR SUPREMACY IN INDIA.

(The "Le Bas" Prize Essay for 1886.)

BY

EDWARD J. RAPSON, B.A.

CLASSICAL FOUNDATION SCHOLAR, AND HUTCHINSON (INDIAN LANGUAGES) STUDENT OF ST. JOHN'S COLLEGE, CAMBRIDGE.

LONDON:
TRÜBNER & CO., LUDGATE HILL.
1887.

TO

MRS. GOLDNEY,

This Essay,

JUDGED WORTHY OF THE PRIZE

INSTITUTED IN HONOUR OF HER FATHER,

THE REV. CHARLES WEBB LE BAS, M.A.,

IS, WITH PROFOUND RESPECT,

Dedicated

BY

THE AUTHOR.

CONTENTS.

"The French fight for glory; . . . but John Bull, who is a reasonable, moral, and reflective character, fights to promote trade, to maintain peace and order on the face of the earth for the good of mankind in general; and, if he has conquered any one, it was to improve his condition in this world, and to secure his welfare in the next."—MAX O'RELL.

ERRATUM.

Page 46, line 24 } *for* "étendu" *read* "entendu."
" 48, " 20 }

THE STRUGGLE BETWEEN ENGLAND AND FRANCE FOR SUPREMACY IN INDIA.

CHAPTER I.

INTRODUCTION.

Literature of the subject—Interest in the period at the present time—Treatment of the period by historians—The earliest accounts chiefly English—Results of recent study of original documents—Scope of the present work.

THE complaint, with which Macaulay begins his essay on Clive, of the want of interest shown by British readers in the history of their own countrymen in India, could not be repeated with anything like equal truth at the present day. Interest in the affairs of India, whether past or present, is certainly still far from general, but it has of late years enormously increased; and this increase has called forth a vast body of literature dealing with every branch of the subject. In Macaulay's time, Orme's "History of the Military Achievements of the British in Indostan" and Mill's "History of British India" were the chief and almost the only works, from which a knowledge of modern Indian history could be gained. Both of these works were excellent in their way; and it says much for their excellence that Mill, as edited by Professor Wilson in 1851, still remains the standard work on the history of British India, taken as a whole, while Orme's history, with its scrupulous accuracy and minuteness of detail, will ever remain the great storehouse of materials for an account of the particular period with which the present essay deals. But neither of these important works was written in a style sufficiently popular to attract the attention of the general reader. At the present time, however, there are very many books dealing with the history of India, whether regarded as a whole, or with special reference to particular periods; and many of these are of a high degree of excellence, while, at the same time, they are written in a most readable style. The difficulty of the reader now is not a lack of books, but the choice of the best.

The period, during which English and French fought for supremacy in India, has only during the last twenty years gained any considerable attention on the part of English readers. This attention it has gained not more by its importance than by the fact that its true history, and especially the history of some of the great men who took part in the struggle, had been until recently perverted; and, in the place of facts, the bare assertions of prejudiced chroniclers were implicitly believed.

The struggle in India was but an episode in the grand struggle between England and France, which lasted through so many centuries. To use the words of Professor Seeley, India was but a "part of the chessboard, on which England and France played out their game of skill." To contemporary Englishmen its importance could not seem very great. A very small space is allotted to it, for instance, in the columns of the "Annual Review." When contrasted with the European affairs of the period, its importance could not be properly appreciated. In the one case, our forefathers saw the two mightiest nations of Europe straining every muscle in a life-and-death contest; they were apt to think of the other as little more than a feud between rival commercial companies, strengthened every now and then by reinforcements from home.

To us, however, as we look back, the scene wears a very different aspect. We live among the gigantic consequences of that apparently insignificant struggle; and, in tracing step by step the wonderful history, which lies between the middle of the eighteenth and the middle of the nineteenth century—the story how, in that period, a foreign mercantile corporation became the supreme rulers of India—our attention cannot fail to be attracted, in an especial manner, to that period of about fifteen years, which was the very crisis of our existence in India.

But the struggle with France was even more than this. As we glance backwards, and examine the course of events then by the light of subsequent experience, we can plainly see that, as surely as defeat would have brought with it perpetual banishment, so surely did victory bring to the victors the necessity of continual progress in the road entered upon. The game was played for annihilation or for empire; although the players, at the time, could not be conscious of the magnitude of the stake. The positions, to which English and French attained during the struggle, were such as to make the continued existence of a French and English power side by side in India an impossibility. The event of the struggle, too, was such as to make the existence of the victorious nation, under the rule of the native powers, equally an impossibility. The weakness of the empire of the Great Mogul was laid bare; the inefficiency of his armies was proved again and again; his utter inability to keep the subordinate powers in control, the constant mutual feuds and jealousies of these subordinate powers, their unanimity in rebellion against the supreme power, whenever opportunity presented itself—all these things were impressed on the minds of the Europeans, who, during the struggle, were brought into contact with the native powers; and the Europeans could not help also seeing how easily such a state of affairs might be used to their own advantage. Prospects so glorious presented themselves, that it was beyond the power of man's nature to resist; but even leaving out of consideration such temptation, it was not possible that the Europeans, now that they had learned their own strength and the weakness of their masters, could ever again resume their former position, in which they had been, to a great extent, subject to the will of native princes. There had been a time, when they would meekly suffer the insult and exaction of the meanest of native powers; but that time was past, and could never come again.

The study of this period, marking as it does the commencement of our empire in India, is highly important. It is, moreover, highly interesting for the reason mentioned above—the remarkable treatment it has received at the hands of historians. The early accounts of the struggle between English and French in India were written chiefly by Englishmen, and founded on the reports of Englishmen, many of whom had taken an active part in the struggle. At that time, national hatred and national prejudice were too strong to allow Englishmen and Frenchmen to form a calm and fair opinion on the actions of one another. Neither nation scrupled to attribute the meanest motives to its rival. In such cases, when we possess the accounts given by both sides, it is usually not difficult to get at the truth, by striking the balance, as it were, between them; but, in this particular instance, circumstances were such that the English accounts at last gained general acceptance, and were regarded as true by both French and English readers. The reason for this lies in the nature of the French accounts, such as they were. All the great Frenchmen, who served in India, wrote "Memoirs" on their return to France; but these memoirs were one and all written with the object of justifying the course followed by their writers while in India. Thus

Dupleix, Bussy, and Lally wrote in defence of themselves, in answer to charges brought against them by the French East India Company or the French Government. Such accounts would naturally be regarded as one-sided. More than this, they were in certain cases directly conflicting. Dupleix and De la Bourdonnais each wrote in his own defence against the accusations of the other; and Law wrote in defence of himself against the charges of Dupleix. Such causes prevented the few early French narratives from being regarded as veracious history, and it was not until at least eighty years after the termination of the war in the Carnatic that any important historical work dealing with this period appeared in France.[1] By this time, the English accounts had attained to the rank of standard works on the subject; and the names of the great French leaders still continued to be associated with much unmerited ignominy. The only Frenchman, for whom the English had conceived any admiration, was M. de la Bourdonnais, the Governor of the Isle of France; and he, without any doubt whatever, after a career, in which he had triumphed over misfortune and adversity in a manner truly wonderful, turned traitor to his own countrymen at the last.

The neglect, with which this period has been treated by French historians, has been frequently commented on; and the cause usually assigned for this neglect is, no doubt, the correct one. The Great Revo-

[1] "L'histoire de la conquête de l'Inde," par le Baron Barchou de Penhoen, Paris, 1844; and "L'Inde," par M. Dubois de Jancigny et M. Xavier Raymond, Paris, 1845.

lution makes a huge gap in French history. It came like a second chaos; and out of this chaos proceeded the elements which constitute the France of to-day. It is back to the First Empire that the French love to trace the origin of their national life. All beyond this they are apt to view with diminished interest; and the short but glorious episode of French achievements in India has been passed by almost unnoticed.

It is gratifying to think, now that the hatred and bigotry, which blinded Englishmen and Frenchmen to everything but the faults of each other, are matters of the past, that the removal of all the misconception and misrepresentation, by which the French name in India suffered for a century, was due, in the first instance, entirely to the efforts of Englishmen. This was done, within the last twenty-five years, by the examination of unpublished and almost forgotten documents.

The keeper of the archives at Pondichery during the war was M. Ariel, who, at his death, bequeathed the papers in his possession to the Bibliothèque Nationale. It was from a study of these Ariel papers, that a writer in the *National Review*, in 1862, was able to give to the world a true account of the part taken by M. Dupleix after the surrender of Madras, in 1746, and of his celebrated quarrel with M. de la Bourdonnais. It was this article in the *National Review*, which suggested to Colonel G. B. Malleson the idea of subjecting the whole period to a thorough examination by the aid of unpublished documents. In addition to the information afforded by the Ariel papers, he was able to throw much light on the subject, through the perusal of papers relating to the East India Company, in the library of the India Office. The results of his investigations were, at first, published periodically in the *Calcutta Review*, during the years 1865–1867. These were subsequently published in the form of a book entitled "The History of the French in India." Of this work it is impossible to speak too highly. It marks a distinct epoch in the study of the period with which it deals, and gives the result of patient historical research clothed in the most readable English. That it was appreciated by French readers was shown by its translation into French by Madame S. le Page, and by the appearance of an excellent French work, which was directly suggested by it, "Dupleix, d'après sa correspondence inédite," by M. Tibulle Hamont. This last work appeared as recently as the year 1881, and is a befitting monument to that great man, whom France neglected to honour during his life, and whose memory was held in dishonour even by his own countrymen for a hundred years after his death. The diligent search, which M. Hamont made in the different French libraries, was amply rewarded, not only by the discovery of the correspondence of Dupleix with his officers, with the officials of the French East India Company, and with his own family, but also by the discovery of an important account of the conquest of the Dekhan written by M. Kerjean, the nephew of Dupleix.

The result of all the above-mentioned investigations has been, in many instances, a complete reversal of opinions previously held. Our faith has suffered a severe shock; and our present danger is the danger of allowing ourselves to be carried too far by the reaction which has set in. In the opinion of the writer of this essay, neither Colonel Malleson nor M. Hamont has been altogether able to resist the temptations to hero-worship. For this M. Hamont has more excuse than Colonel Malleson: the former is a biographer, the latter an historian. In the course of this essay instances will be pointed out, in which Colonel Malleson, while nobly defending the cause of French honour and French courage, has, in the opinion of the writer, forgotten to do justice to the English. The failures of the English to keep in the path of strict honesty, in their dealings with the native powers, invariably bring down the wrath of Colonel Malleson, and with justice. Such an affair as the forgery of Watson's signature by Clive (if true—and it would appear that there was some doubt on this point) rightly excites the ire of every honest man; but surely Colonel Malleson, if regarding the matter at all from a moral standpoint, should be equally severe on the transgressions of the French in this respect; and they were by no means free from such, although to a reader, whose only guide was Colonel Malleson, it would seem almost as if they were. Colonel Malleson blushes for Clive's lapse; while he quotes with approbation the conduct of his favourite, Dupleix, when, to ordinary mortals, it seems equally blameworthy. To take one instance only, with regard to the course pursued by the envoys of

Dupleix, when Násir Jang, the claimant to the throne of the Dekhan, favoured by the English, appeared for the moment victorious, and without a rival; Colonel Malleson says ("History of the French in India," p. 251): "To favour their negotiations, they had recourse to those wiles which they had learned from the Asiatic princes, and which they now showed they could use more skilfully than their masters. Thus they took credit for the defeat of d'Auteuil (their own general!) . . . All this time (*i.e.*, while they were trying to come to terms with the Nizam himself) these same agents intrigued with the chiefs of the Nizam's army, especially with the Patan Nawabs of Kuddapa, Kurnool, and Savanore, and succeeded in establishing with these and others relations of a confidential nature." Truly, these disciples had learned to outwit their masters; but so had Clive, and by precisely similar means—duplicity and deceit of the very worst kind; and it is not easy to see on what principles a different verdict should be given in each case.

The fact is, that stirring events, like the struggle between English and French for supremacy in India, excite to their utmost all the deep-seated principles of human action. Such times always produce great men; and great warriors and great diplomatists are, as a rule, men whose faults also are great. Contemporary historians treat them each in accordance with the bias of his own mind. Such has always been the lot of men like Cæsar, or Cromwell, or Napoleon. Such, in subsequent Anglo-Indian history, was the lot of Dalhousie. To deliberate partisans fairness is impossible; a true verdict, in such matters, can only be given by an unbiassed posterity.

If the quotation of instances such as that mentioned above should produce in this essay the appearance of patriotic partiality, it will be an appearance only. With the adequate materials, which we now possess for forming an opinion on the subject, no one can doubt any longer that, in point of personal bravery, the French were at least our equals; in tact and foresight, certainly our superiors. The causes, which produced our ultimate success and their failure, had nothing to do with these: they were, to a great extent, beyond the control of either the English or the French settlers in India.

Anything like a complete record of even the most important events during the war would be beyond the scope of the present essay. The object here will be principally to describe the position held in India by English and French, both in relation to each other and to the native powers, previous to the struggle; to point out the policy, in accordance with which the actions of each had, up to that time, been directed; to sum up, at convenient intervals, the influence, which the course of events during the war, and the action of the controlling powers in Europe, had in changing the status and the policy of each; and, in this way, to seek for an explanation of those causes, which led ultimately to the triumph of the one and to the downfall of the other.

In addition to works previously mentioned, the following have been used:—"British Power in India," Auber; "History of the Britannic Constitution," Creasy; "British Rule in India," James; "History of the East India Company," Kaye; Macaulay's "Essay on Clive," and Malleson's "Life of Clive;" "Final French Struggles," Malleson; "History of India," Marshman; "British Rule in India," Martineau; "Manual of Indian History," Meadows Taylor; "India on the Eve of the British Conquest," Owen; "Expansion of England," Seeley; "Empire in India," Torrens; "Early Records of British India," Talboys Wheeler; "Historical Sketches of the Kingdom of Mysore," Wilks; and articles in the "Cyclopædia of India," the "Encyclopædia Britannica," and the "Biographie Générale."

The question of the spelling of oriental names of persons and places is one of considerable difficulty. The two extremes are the purely phonetic spelling of Orme and the rigid system of transliteration (as far as possible with the Roman alphabet) adopted by Malleson in his "Life of Clive." Both of these systems are open to the same objection at the present day, in so far as they frequently make words difficult of recognition to the general reader. It was thought best, therefore, to follow a system similar to that adopted by some well-known work on Indian history, which effects a compromise in this respect; and the work chosen was Elphinstone's "History of India," as edited by Professor Cowell (sixth edition).

CHAPTER II.

THE EVE OF THE STRUGGLE.

European settlers in India: Portuguese, Dutch, English, and French—Political state of India—Dissolution of the Mogul Empire—English and French East India Companies—General attitude of natives towards settlers—Policy of the English Company purely mercantile—One short period an exception—Different views on this point—Friendly relations with native powers of French, under Martin, Lenoir, and Dumas—Affair of Kárikál—The French resist the Mahrattas—Dupleix—Difference of status occupied by French and English—Possible reasons for this.

In the year 1740, six years before the outbreak of war between the English and French in India, these two nations alone, out of the four chief European nations, who had embarked in Eastern enterprise, continued to hold any considerable power. The Portuguese—the first on the scene—had for a century maintained a complete monopoly of Eastern trade, and had raised up on the continent of India itself a power such as none of their European successors attained for a century and a half after their downfall. But their glory had long ago departed. The bigotry and intolerance and cruelty, which characterised the successors of d'Albuquerque, had long ago met with their just reward. The Dutch, who succeeded, in like manner failed to maintain the enormous power which they had once gained. They brought about their own ruin by a flagrant abuse of the monopoly, which they had wrested from the Portuguese. Next came the English, who, at this time, still continued to keep in their own hands the greater share of the traffic between Europe and India; and, some sixty years after the English, came the French, whose commercial success, while not equalling that of the English, was still such as to make them formidable rivals.

Up to this time, English and French had existed side by side in India, without coming into serious collision, for more than seventy years, although England and France had been at war with each other for a considerable portion of that period. The settlers of the two nations had hitherto pursued entirely independent courses. The policy adopted by either side towards the rulers and inhabitants of the country, in which the settlements stood, was neither imitated from nor influenced by that pursued by the other, and the result of this was an important difference between the nature of English and French power and policy in India, which very greatly influenced the character of the subsequent struggle. In fact, this distinction, which was doubtless to a great extent the outcome of circumstances acting on the different national temperaments, made the contest an unequal one at the very outset, by placing the combatants on entirely different levels; and, had it not been for the preponderating influence of external causes—causes beyond the control of the settlers, whether English or French—the result of the contest would, in all probability, not have been what it was. It will be necessary, therefore, to gain a general idea, first, of the political state of India at this period, and, secondly, of the history of English and French in India up to this date.

At no time, of which we possess any historical record, did India constitute "a conscious political whole."[1] Throughout history the term "India" is little more than a geographical expression, under which is included a greater or less number of distinct states possessing a varying share of power and independence. For a few years, during the reigns of Akber and his immediate successors, the majority of these states were linked together by conquest, and formed a great consolidated power, having its forces centered in the throne of Delhi. This was the empire of the Great Mogul, as our ancestors termed it, and a very mighty empire it was; but, even in its most powerful days, there remained Hindú states which it could never conquer, and which paid it no allegiance, or an allegiance in name only. Such a state was that of the Mahrattas —a power which, from small beginnings, had grown until now, on the eve of the French and English struggle, it was feared more than any other power in India. The Mahrattas had already more than once dictated terms to the Emperor of Delhi. They were one of the chief causes of the disintegration of the Mogul Empire. The other chief cause was the great

[1] Much of this account of the political state of India at this period is borrowed from Professor Seeley's "Expansion of England."

Persian invasion under Nádir Sháh in 1739, during which the Persian troops had occupied and devastated Delhi, and taken the Emperor, Mohammed Sháh, prisoner. Nádir Sháh retired only through the persuasion of an enormous bribe. Such attacks from within and without severely tasked the central power, and lessened its control over the subordinate powers. Of this fact the subordinate powers were nothing loth to take advantage; and, at the time of which we are writing, each of the chief subdivisions of the vast Mogul Empire constituted practically an independent power.

These principal subdivisions were called "súbahs," and their rulers "súbahdárs" or viceroys. In discussing the struggle between the English and French in India, we shall have occasion to mention two of these—the súbahdár of the Dekhan and the súbahdár of Bengal. Under the rule of the súbahdárs were included various subordinate powers, called by different names in different parts of India; and, just as the súbahdárs, when they felt themselves strong enough, threw off allegiance to the Emperor of Delhi, so did the nawábs and rájas, when an opportunity presented itself, throw off allegiance to their súbahdár. Of these minor subordinate powers, the one with whom we shall have most to do is the nawáb of the Carnatic, in whose dominions by far the greater part of the struggle was fought out. This nawáb, too, was practically independent, and the post, which was theoretically in the gift of the súbahdár of the Dekhan. had become hereditary.

Thus, at this period of Indian history, might was right. The various subordinate powers were divided one against the other, and were unanimous only in rebellion against the supreme power. Beyond this there was no common feeling of nationality, no common bond of religion. A state of almost complete anarchy was universal, and everything was decided by force or intrigue. It was only the existence of such a state of things which rendered possible the mighty empire which Europeans have established in India.

It was no uncommon thing for mere soldiers of fortune to fight their way to the highest positions in the empire, and, such being the case, it would have been nothing incredible, if at this period a band of European settlers, united for the purpose of conquest, had gained for themselves considerable political power in India. Indeed the Portuguese had long ago shown the extent to which this was possible. Up to this time, however, neither French nor English had attained to any such power. Their settlements were in no sense of the word political settlements. They were the possessions not of the French or of the English crown, but of the French or of the English East India Company; and these companies were in dependence on the home governments only in the sense that the right of exclusive trade to the East, which they claimed, was founded upon the authority of royal or parliamentary charters. Such hatred as existed between the servants of the two companies in India was due to commercial and not to national jealousy.

As might naturally be expected, the histories of the French and English settlements in India, founded and governed as they were in imitation of their rivals the Dutch, have much in common with each other. The ruling idea of both was to monopolise, as far as possible, all Indo-European trade, and they had, therefore, the same kind of difficulties to contend with, in their endeavours to prevent encroachment, from whatsoever source, on this—as they regarded it—their peculiar privilege. At first the sole concern of each was traffic, and nothing was farther from their thoughts than the idea of extensive territorial possession on their own account. They held the land, on which their factories were built, either as tenants of the native powers, in consideration of the payment of an annual rent, or as their own property by gift or purchase. In every case they were directly subject to the native prince, in whose territory such land was situated. They were tolerated for the sole reason that their commerce brought an accession of wealth to the states in which they settled. The native powers, however jealous they might feel towards the settlers, were too wise to drive them away altogether; but, short of this, they as a rule made the servants of both companies feel their power to the uttermost by imposing exorbitant taxes and transit duties, and sometimes by enforcing large donations. That such an attitude as this should be generally taken up by the native powers towards the settlers seems after all only natural. The fact is important only in so far as it contributed to what may be called the formation of the characters of the English and French peoples in India. To start with, there would naturally exist a want of sympathy with the natives on the part of the Europeans; and the Europeans might either accept this want of sympathy as inevitable and as not to be overcome, or they might attempt to come to a better understanding with the natives by respecting native customs and prejudices. As will be seen, the English, on the whole, followed the former course, and the French the latter; and the importance of this difference is seen from the fact that, on the eve of the struggle, the English still held aloof, as far as possible, from all intercourse with native princes, while the French had gained not only the friendship of the royal family, in whose territory their chief settlement, Pondichery, was situated, but also the respect of its foes.

The history of the English in India, from the incorporation of the East India Company, in the year 1600, until the outbreak of war with the French—a period of nearly a century and a half—is little more than the history of a mercantile body attempting to gain and hold a monopoly. In this attempt they were brought into collision with both Portuguese and Dutch; but it will be unnecessary to relate their various struggles with these, since their relations, whether with the natives or with the French, were in no way influenced thereby. With the notable exception of a short period, which will be discussed hereafter, it may be said that they consistently followed, as far as circumstances allowed them, the advice given by Sir Thomas Roe, in the year 1615, "to seek their profit at sea and in quiet trade, and not to affect garrisons and land wars in India." The object which brought them to India was trade, and on this they concentrated all their energies. For this reason they not only abstained from siding with any of the native parties in their struggles with one another, but they even submitted to much unjust and vexatious treatment which, otherwise, they might have felt strongly tempted to resent.

This fact has led some writers to speak in disparaging terms of the English settlers as a set of cravens, who would submit to any imposition rather than run the slightest risk of losing any of their trade. But this is putting the case unfairly. Their great wish was, indeed, to be allowed to go their own way in peace, but they showed again and again that there were limits to their endurance of unjust treatment even to secure this. That they were quite prepared to hold their own was shown in 1664, when the Mahṛatta general, Sivají, attacked Surat. On this occasion the natives fled in despair, and the only opposition offered to Sivají was by the English at that place, who undertook to defend not only themselves but also the natives—a piece of bravery in gratitude for which the Emperor Aurungzíb remitted the greater portion of the duties, which he claimed on the English traffic.

Strangely enough, the very opposite opinion has been held by some writers,[1] and the English settlers

[1] *e.g.*, Torrens, "Empire in Asia."

represented, not as traders wholly absorbed in buying and selling, but as deliberate aggressors whose chief aim, from the very first, and throughout their career, was the attainment of power in India. How such an opinion can be compatible with a knowledge of this period of history it is quite impossible to understand.

The short period alluded to above, as affording an exception to the usual course of the policy of the English in India, lasts from about 1685 to 1690. For some reason or other, a fit of ambition seized the directors of the Company at this time, and the English in India assumed an offensive attitude towards the native powers. The ruling spirits in this movement were the brothers Sir Josiah and Sir John Child, the former being head of the Court of Directors at home, and the latter in sole command of an expedition sent out from England. There seems to be little doubt that the war was, to a very great extent, the work of these two men. The pretext was the unjust and cruel conduct of the native powers towards the English in Bengal. This was without doubt a real and serious grievance; but it is equally certain that the expedition was prompted by an ambitious project of establishing an actual English power in Bengal itself, no less than by the desire to obtain satisfaction, or to bring the native powers to equal terms. As it happened, the expedition, from one cause and another, after a small share of success, failed entirely. The wrath of the Great Mogul, the Emperor Aurungzíb, was fully kindled, and the English were expelled from every part of India. They were permitted to return only by making "the most abject submissions." They had received a lesson, which they did not forget for very many years.

It is from this very point, strange to say, that Mill dates the aggressive policy of the English. After describing their utter defeat, he says, "It was now laid down as a determinate object of policy, that independence was to be established in India, and dominion acquired." As a matter of fact, the whole history of the Company for the next fifty years is a direct contradiction of this. The only instance adduced by Mill in support of his statement is the purchase and fortification of Fort St. David. If this proves anything, it proves that the English had been taught, by recent events, how precarious their existence in India was, and that they thought it necessary to possess some stronghold on the western coast, to which they might escape, if Madras were at any time attacked by an overwhelming force. In spite of the celebrated instructions of the Directors, which Mill quotes, and which have been quoted since so often,[1] nothing is more certain than that the English in India, whatever may have been the views of their masters at home, ceased to make any such attempts to gain extensive territorial

1 "The increase of our revenue is the subject of our care as much as our trade: it is that must maintain our force, when twenty accidents may interrupt our trade: it is that must make us a nation in India; without that we are a great number of interlopers united by charter, fit only to trade where nobody thinks it their interest to prevent us."

possession, and relapsed once again into their original position of merchants and merchants only. Referring to the document quoted by Mill, Marshman describes it as the "dying indication" of the "sudden spasm of ambition," with which the Directors had been seized at this time.

Certain it is that from this time onwards, the English continued to regard any scheme of extensive territorial possession with positive aversion. This conduct was by no means caused by any lofty ideal of national morality, but by the plain matter-of-fact consideration that an aggressive policy was risky, and just as likely to result in failure as in success. They were plain business men, whose one object was to make for themselves fortunes sufficient to enable them to return to their native country, and to spend the remainder of their lives there in peace and comfort. They failed to see in what manner the actual possession of numerous places in India would benefit their commerce. The position they held as tenants, or, at all events, as subjects of the Great Mogul, was, in their opinion, far preferable provided that they were free from molestation. They wished only to have factories—which were nothing more than warehouses and counting-houses combined—and even of these they wished to have as few as they conveniently could. The establishment of new factories was always accompanied with much grumbling at the hard necessity. As for forts and armed troops, they dispensed with both as far as they possibly could; and, when these were necessary to protect their goods from robbery at the hands of organised bodies of natives, or to protect their trade against other Europeans, or, perhaps most of all, against the "interlopers," as they styled those English adventurers who, from time to time, made bold to infringe on their monopoly, they never allowed them to rise above the minimum state of efficiency compatible with their safety. Indeed, at one time, the old Company nearly lost its monopoly altogether for this very reason. One of the arguments urged against it and in favour of Courten's Association in 1635, was that the former had neglected to build forts. So very remote does interference in native affairs seem to have been from the minds of the English, that, during the war of succession at the end of Sháh Jehán's reign, they actually imported from England stores of warlike ammunition, thinking that such would be likely, at that time, to find a good market. While their imagination failed to detect any advantage to be gained by territorial possession, or by a policy of interference in native affairs, such as the French adopted to gain this end, they were quite awake to the fact that failure in such a project would certainly bring disaster to their trade, and, in all probability, eternal banishment of themselves from the peninsula of Hindostán.

On the eve of the struggle between English and French in India, the English had had settlements there for about one hundred and forty years. The French had been there for little more than half that time. We have seen that the English hitherto had conducted themselves merely as traders in a foreign land, that they had entered into no alliance with a native power, and that they had not made one step towards acquiring for themselves territorial rule in India. Let us see how the French had conducted themselves in this respect during their much shorter sojourn there.

In the year 1674, ten years after the foundation of the French East India Company, the French bought from the Bíjapúr government the land, on which the town of Pondichery stands. Three years afterwards, Pondichery was threatened by the Mahratta force under Sivají, but was saved by the judicious measures adopted by the governor, François Martin. The tact displayed by the French on this occasion gained for them the admiration and friendship of the ruler of Bíjapúr. Not many years after this, the kingdom of Bíjapúr was incorporated with the Mogul Empire, and placed under the rule of the nawáb of the Carnatic. The first nawáb of the Carnatic, who assumed anything like independent power, was Sádat Alla Khán. With him the French established friendly relations, but it was with his nephew and successor, Dóst Alí, and with his son-in-law, Chandá Sáhéb, that they established that firm alliance, which so greatly affected their future. Chandá Sáhéb especially was an enthusiastic admirer of the French, and showed, by his subsequent conduct, that he both appreciated their good qualities and had, at the same time, detected their desire for power in India. When this desire on the part of the French first arose it is impossible to say quite exactly, but it was certainly early in their career in India.

This policy, which the French adopted, of making native alliance the means by which they might ultimately gain their ends, was above all things unaggressive in character; and so it remained until the time of Dupleix. Every fresh addition to the power of the French under Martin, Lenoir, and Dumas, was made without striking a blow, and, in the case of the two first, without making an enemy. During the time that M. Benoît Dumas held the office of governor-general of the French settlements in India, he maintained a close friendship with Dóst Alí, the nawáb of the Carnatic, and continued to extend this friendship to his family after his death. By means of this friendship he obtained from the Emperor of Delhi, Mohammed Sháh, through the mediation of Dóst Alí, the permission to coin money at Pondichery—an item of no small importance in the growth of French commerce in India.

The idea entertained by the natives of French power was even now considerable. During the struggle in 1738 for the sovereignty of Tanjore, Sahújí, the eldest living son of the late rája, sent to implore the assistance of the French, offering to grant them, in return, the town of Kárikál, and a considerable portion of the neighbouring territory. Dumas aided him with money and arms, and he was successful; but, like a true Oriental, he evaded the fulfilment of his promise.

Here was certainly a great temptation for the French to employ force; but their friendship with the family of Dóst Alí saved them from the necessity. Chandá Sáhéb, who was at this time the rája of Trichinopoly, came forward and offered to make Sahújí fulfil his promise and hand over Kárikál to the French. He was as good as his word, and, early in 1739, Kárikál became a French possession, without the French in India having struck a single blow to obtain it. Sahújí himself hastened to make friends with them, and sent them a ratification of the treaty, and an order to the inhabitants to obey their new masters. Soon after this, Sahújí was driven from the throne by his brother, Prátab Sing, who likewise made a bid for the continuance of French favours, by adding to the territory given to them, and even advising them to fortify the towns in their new possessions.

The affair of Kárikál is a good instance of the policy pursued by the French governors of this period. They were keen enough to see that diplomacy was all that was needed to gain everything they could want, and they were prudent enough not to let their anger at any time lead them to attack any of the native powers. They clearly saw that it was their best policy to play a waiting game.

During the same year, an event happened, which placed the French in a somewhat different position. As they had never of themselves attacked a native power, so they had hitherto remained free from actual attack by a native power. They gained their first experience of this, just as the English had, at the hands of the Mahrattas—an enemy dreaded above all throughout the length and breadth of Hindostan. These Mahrattas had made another incursion into the Carnatic, and had slain in battle the nawáb and his second son. The eldest son, Safder Alí, and the son-in-law of the nawáb, Chandá Sáhéb, had not been present with their forces; but thinking that the arms of the Mahrattas would now be turned against them, and doubting their ability to make an effectual resistance, they sought some place of refuge for their families and treasures. Pondichery occurred to both of them, and they asked consent to place there the one his mother, and the other his wife. Here was a dilemma. On the one hand, the friendship of the French with the nawáb had been productive of too many advantages to be lightly ignored, while, on the other, this protection afforded to his family was certain to provoke an attack of the Mahrattas. Dumas chose the latter alternative, and presented a bold front to the enemy, which seems to have inspired these hardy warriors with admiration for French pluck. On the first occasion, the Mahratta general seems to have contented himself with threatening Pondichery and demanding tribute. Both the threat and the demand were calmly ignored; but, about the end of the same year, the Mahrattas again returned, in accordance with a disgraceful understanding with Safder Alí, whose interest it was now to have Chandá Sáhéb out of his way. While on this expedition against Chandá Sáhéb, the Mahrattas took the opportunity of carrying into practice their previous threats against the French. Again Dumas was resolute. In fine, the Mahrattas raised the siege and withdrew, and the French had gained more prestige than they could have gained by the most brilliant victory. The French had made their name; and the mean opinion which the natives were previously inclined to hold of Europeans in general perhaps only tended to augment the admiration they felt for this one nation now. This resistance of Dumas may be said to have created a prestige, without the aid of which the glorious career of the French subsequently would scarcely have been possible. In the case of peoples, and especially in the case of oriental peoples, so disorganised, so split up into innumerable factions, so entirely devoid of any bond to keep them together, nothing conduces to success so much as prestige. This alone, for instance, accounts for some of the most remarkable successes of Clive. The prestige, which the French had now gained, was, moreover, of no ordinary kind. They had run an enormous risk against a most formidable foe, not from any compulsion, but simply because they had determined to stand by their friends. They had shown a degree of courage, joined to a nobility of mind, such as the natives could never have seen before, but which none are more capable of appreciating than Orientals. In the state of universal insecurity, each petty conqueror had quite enough to do to look after his own interests, and, as a rule, did not scruple to throw his friends overboard when they had ceased to be of service to him.

Henceforth the French occupy a distinctly higher

status, and are by all recognised as by no means the least of the powers of India. Thanks, accompanied by the most valuable presents, came to the French from all the great native powers, and, what is most significant as indicating the relation of the French to the native powers, the Emperor of Delhi himself conferred on the Governor of Pondichery and his successors the rank and title of nawáb, and the high dignity of the command of 4500 horse.

Soon after this Dumas resigned, and left all the honours he had gained for his successor, Joseph François Dupleix, the Governor of Chandernagor, a man who possessed an equal knowledge of the state of native affairs, and joined to this an ambition even greater. His promptitude and boldness formed a contrast to the cautious policy of Dumas. The policy of Dumas had been essentially one of peace, of interference only when interference was safe, and of resistance only when the honour of the French name called for it. Dupleix mingled more freely in the affairs of native princes, and tended more to take up an independent position. The French had hitherto acted the *rôle* of humble allies of a native prince. These positions were shortly to be completely reversed. Dumas had laid the foundation of French power in India: it remained for Dupleix to raise the superstructure. The characters of these two men seem to have been admirably adapted to the work each had to do.

Dupleix was strongly convinced of the importance of gaining the sympathy of the natives, and took pains to impress upon them the fact that, in his capacity of nawáb, he too was an officer of the Great Mogul. He adopted the Eastern mode of life, and paid and received visits among the native princes with the greatest punctiliousness. In this way he learnt the real weakness of every native state, disguised though it might be by pomp and display. By skilful and patient diplomacy, he gained a complete knowledge of every little move in the intricate game of intrigue, which was going on all around, and saw that it would be possible to take advantage of such a state of things for the purpose of founding a French empire in India. In this work Dupleix found an enthusiastic assistant in his wife, whose intimate acquaintance with the native languages proved of the greatest service.

It will be seen, then, that the positions of English and French in India, with reference to the native powers, though identical at first, had, in course of time, become as widely different as possible. There is, no doubt, much in national temperament to account for this. The English, slow and sure, turned away from an ambitious dream, the fulfilment of which might be a future possibility, to reap the certain advantages of material wealth in the present. The French, impulsive and sanguine, no sooner saw before them a glorious prospect, than they subordinated to its attainment every act of their existence in India.

Besides this, there is one fact in connection with the foundation of the French East India Company by Colbert, in the year 1664, on which little stress has been laid, but which may not unreasonably be regarded as having, at the very outset, influenced their subsequent career in India, by promoting the development of those characteristics which distinguished them from the English. This was the proclamation of Louis XIV., to the effect that a man of noble birth suffered no degradation by engaging in the East Indian trade. The primary motive for this proclamation was to encourage the *noblesse* to subscribe to the East India Company; but may it not also have produced another effect? When we consider what the state of the French nobility was at this time, the number of its members, its rigid exclusiveness, and the fact that for these reasons many of its members were doomed to lives of idleness and, at the same time, of almost abject poverty, we can well understand that full advantage was taken of this outlet for its energies. Many young scions of the nobility, who had no career to look forward to in France, proceeded to India in the service of the Company; and may not this sprinkling of men, who had been taught all their previous life to scorn the pursuits of commerce, and to look upon the career of a statesman as the ideal of life, help to explain the fact that the French had fully conceived the idea of political power at a very early period of their career in India?

CHAPTER III.

THE OUTBREAK OF WAR.

Ill-feeling between the two Companies—Extension of the Austrian war of succession to the settlements in India—Prospect of war viewed differently by English and French—The French try to obtain a treaty of neutrality—An English fleet despatched for the Indian seas—The nawáb of the Carnatic prohibits the English from attacking Pondichery—Commencement of the actual struggle—Division of the war into three periods—The scene of action.

ALL this time the English in India had remained stationary, steadily plodding on, wholly intent on fortune-making. It may well be supposed that these peaceful traders viewed with extreme alarm the ambitious projects of the French, and many were the complaints on this subject which they made to their masters at home.

The state of feeling which existed at this time may be imagined, if we consider that this last source of irritation was superadded to the hatred begotten of commercial jealousy, which had always existed between the two peoples in India. Want of enterprise characterised both companies; and this, joined to the commercial systems which were followed by each, and which were, in certain points, radically wrong, kept them both in a state of penury. Numbers of fortunes were made, indeed, by members of the companies; but neither of the companies themselves was, at this period, a great success. Neither company had the insight to see that the remedy lay, for the most part, in its own hands. Each attributed its failure in commerce to its inability to maintain a strict monopoly of the traffic between Europe and India. The result was that, instead of reforming its own trade-system, each thought the great end to be obtained was the destruction of the commerce of its rival; and, to obtain this end, neither neglected to employ every means in its power, whether honourable or dishonourable. Rival traders thus situated are perhaps, without exception, the most unscrupulous of mortals. The utter want of good faith and common honesty—not to speak of open or insidious attacks on the material wealth of each other—which characterised the dealings of all the early East India Companies, whether Portuguese, Dutch, English, or French, almost passes belief; and perhaps the degradation of baseness was never greater than in the case of the English and French during the few years before they came to an open rupture. Neither scrupled to encourage and bribe bands of outlaws to inflict what damage they could on the other; each held out rewards to the servants of the other to desert; and both were continually doing their best to persuade native powers to harass their rivals by unjust laws, or by exorbitant taxes, and so to make their position on the continent of India unendurable.

Such a state of feeling, existing on the eve of the

struggle, no doubt increased the bitterness with which it was carried on; but was not, in itself, the direct cause of the war between English and French in India. The direct cause was the outbreak of the Austrian war of succession, after the death of the Emperor Charles VI., in 1740. In this war the English and French first took part as auxiliaries on opposite sides, but eventually became the principals in the war. The war of the Austrian succession itself was nothing but a pretext, such as England and France never failed, in those days, to take advantage of, "the actual end desired by either party being the attainment of complete mastery in all points, whether as regarded political ascendancy in Europe, transatlantic dominion, trading monopolies, or maritime power."[1]

Even as early as the year 1741, the news, that England and France were at war, had reached India, and the probability of an extension of the war to the settlements of the two nations in India was rumoured. Such a probability was entertained with very different feelings by each. Such an event would be cordially welcomed by the English, who saw in it the opportunity, for which they longed, to make an attempt to put a stop to what they considered as French encroachment. From a military point of view, they were almost powerless of themselves; but the war would bring to their aid British ships-of-war and troops. They regarded their very existence in India as seriously imperilled by French ambition. It was probable that the question

[1] Martin, "British Colonies."

would have to be settled sooner or later by an appeal to arms, and no opportunity more suitable than the present was likely to occur. The French, on the other hand, dreaded nothing more at this time. Until recently they had not taken into their calculations the possibility of war with the English; and most of their possessions were inadequately defended. It is true, that, on the first rumour of the probable outbreak of war in India, an effort was made to render the French settlements more capable of defence; but this effort was, on the whole, at least as much hindered as assisted by the French government and the Directors of the French East India Company. Their chief settlement, Pondichery, remained ill fortified; and although Dupleix, immediately on his appointment as governor, had set himself energetically to remedy this defect, yet it was two years after the outbreak of the war before the fortifications he had planned were completed, and Pondichery was in a position to defend itself against a European enemy. The French, moreover, had much to lose in case of a defeat. They were in the course of raising an empire by other means. They had without doubt long ago dreamed of the possibility of driving the English out of India altogether; but they had not proposed to effect this by an actual conflict with them, at all events until their own power was such as to leave the English little chance of successful resistance. Their grand idea was power by means of native alliance, of making France a great power in India by the side of the native powers. The extension of the European war to India simply upset all their calculation for the time.

Similar to the views held by their subjects in India were the views held by the controlling powers at home. The cabinet of Versailles proposed to the English government a convention of neutrality between the two companies. This proposal was, however, rejected; and, in 1745, an English fleet was despatched for the Indian seas. The French company seem to have made so sure of obtaining a treaty of neutrality on the part of the two companies, that they actually wrote to Dupleix, ordering him to reduce expenditure, as much as possible, and, above all things, to expend nothing further on fortification.

Here was seen the real evil, of a body of men in Europe, absolutely ignorant and careless of Indian affairs, beyond what concerned their own commerce, having supreme control in all matters relating to the Indian settlements. It was impossible for such men to appreciate the causes, which, at this particular time, made the English eager for a war, in spite of the fact that war would, for a time at least, greatly hinder their trade. It was only by bold disobedience to their orders, by pushing forward the work of fortification with all possible speed, and by supplying from his own fortune the sums which the Company withdrew, that Dupleix saved French power in India. At the same time Dupleix himself tried every means of bringing about a convention of neutrality; but to such a proposal Mr. Morse, who was, at this time, the English governor of Madras, could not agree. The instructions from home were quite definite, and it was not in his power to dispute them.

Having failed, then, to obtain a treaty of neutrality with the English, the French in India, with their chief settlement ill fortified, found themselves in extreme peril. The English fleet under Commodore Barnet was on its way, and it was well known that its instructions were, if possible, to annihilate French commerce. The French government had indeed ordered M. de la Bourdonnais, the governor of the Isle of France, to proceed with a fleet to the assistance of Pondichery; but, almost at the last moment, news was brought to Dupleix that de la Bourdonnais had received instructions to send all his fleet home to France. With this news, the last shadow of hope seemed to have fled.

But now were reaped the firstfruits of that policy of friendly alliance which previous French governors had established with the nawábs of the Carnatic. At the present time the nawáb was Anwár-ud-dín, and to him the French appealed, as feudal lord of both English and French in the Carnatic, to prohibit the English from attacking their settlements. Anwár-ud-dín turned a ready ear to their request, and sent to inform the Governor of Madras that the English settlement there should atone for any injury done to his French subjects. Governor Morse replied as before, that his instructions from home were imperative; but the case was not the same now as it was when he had urged the same plea in answer to the request of Dupleix for a treaty of neutrality. Anwár-ud-dín answered that it mattered not to him from whom the instructions came. All who came to the Coromandel Coast were *ipso facto* his subjects, and would refuse obedience to him at their peril. He, however, promised that he would, in like manner, prevent the French from making any future attack on the English settlements.

The English were intimidated by the threat of Anwár-ud-dín, and Pondichery, a place unprotected by a fleet or by proper fortifications, a place which Barnet's squadron could have taken in a very short time, without any risk to itself, was saved. The enormous disadvantage, at which the English had placed themselves by their utter ignorance of native affairs, was nowhere seen more strikingly than in this instance. They had been content to remain in the belief, which their fathers had held, that the powers of the Great Mogul were invincible. The French, on the other hand, while mingling with native princes, had initiated themselves in all their rivalries and intrigues, and had fully learned the weakness which these rivalries and intrigues produced. A very short time after this, Anwár-ud-dín, in a temporary fit of rage, threatened the French in a somewhat similar manner, and, moreover, had begun to carry his threat into practice with a vast army. Far from submitting, Dupleix ordered a small band of 230 Frenchmen and 700 Sepoys, under a young officer named Paradis, to cut right through this vast army, said to number 10,000, and the result was one of the most complete routs on record.

Orme says, "The rudeness of the military art in Indostan can scarce be imagined but by those who have seen it. The infantry consists of a multitude of people assembled together, without regard to rank and file." This fact was perfectly well known to Dupleix, who could easily take advantage of it. It was either not known to Morse, or, if known, its importance was not appreciated; and so he and the rest of the Madras council meekly bowed to the threat of Anwár-ud-dín, and the strong squadron of Barnet had nothing to do but to occupy itself in the capture of stray French merchantmen utterly incapable of offering any strong resistance.

It is from this point that we may most conveniently date the commencement of the actual struggle between English and French in India. In one form or another, this struggle may be said to have extended over a period lasting until the end of the eighteenth century; but the period of the struggle for supremacy, properly so called, is much more confined. It lasted only about fifteen years—from 1746 till 1761. By the fall of Pondichery in this last year, French power in India was completely overthrown, and the question of supremacy may be said to have been settled once for all. France indeed made subsequent efforts to reopen the question, and for a short period—from 1781–1783—a portion of our empire in Southern India was seriously imperilled; but these efforts could scarcely, under any circumstances, have proved completely successful, since British power was, by this time, too firmly planted in India to be easily rooted up. They are, however, sufficiently important, as regards the amount of damage they inflicted on British power in the East, to call for special notice in connection with our subject.

The whole course of the struggle for supremacy naturally divides itself into three periods, the divisions being marked by two unsuccessful attempts, on the part of the controlling powers at home, to make a lasting peace between the French and English settlers in India. The first period extends from the commencement of the war until the treaty of Aix-la-Chapelle in 1748, by which an attempt was made to place the combatants in the positions they had respectively occupied before the outbreak of war. This attempt was a complete failure, and our second period begins almost immediately after the treaty of Aix-la-Chapelle, and lasts until the treaty of Pondichery in 1754. This second period begins with the renewal of the contest in another form—that of an indirect struggle through the medium of native allies—and ends with the recall of Dupleix from India, and an attempt, on the part of France, to abandon his imperial policy, and, in its place, to inaugurate a policy whose chief feature was to be non-interference in native affairs. After a hollow peace, during which the treaty of Pondichery was violated again and again by both sides, a direct war between English and French commenced again, in consequence of the outbreak of the Seven Years' War in 1756; and our third period extends from this time until the overthrow of the French in 1761.

The scene of action, during the first two periods of the war, is the Carnatic, and, during the second period, it will be necessary also to take a glimpse at the progress of French power in the Dekhan. This, although really outside the struggle, is important, as being the most extensive development of French power in India. In the third period, the scene shifts for a time to Bengal, and then returns to the Carnatic.

As has been indicated before, anything like a detailed account of the events of these three periods would be out of place in an essay like the present. The problem before us may be stated thus: given certain historical facts, to formulate the causes which produced them. An attempt has therefore been made, first of all, to determine accurately the precise positions, which English and French held in India, at the time when the struggle between them began; and, for the future, events will be noticed only in so far as they may be regarded as modifying these positions.

CHAPTER IV.

FIRST PERIOD OF THE WAR.

French fleet under M. de la Bourdonnais—Action with the English fleet—The nawáb refuses to prohibit the French attack on Madras—Fall of Madras—Quarrel between Dupleix and de la Bourdonnais—Its results—Battle of St. Thomé—The superiority of European arms and discipline shown—French attacks on Fort St. David—The English lay siege to Pondichery—Peace declared—Summary of first period—Object of terms in the treaty of Aix-la-Chapelle relating to India—Temptations to Europeans to engage in the affairs of native powers—Number of European troops in India—Alteration in positions of English and French.

THE first attack of the English had, as we have seen, been diverted from its proper object. Pondichery, if attacked by Barnet's squadron, must have fallen; and the fall of Pondichery must have been fatal to French power in India, both commercial and political. The first blow might have finished the war; but the grand opportunity was lost, and the tide of fortune now turned.

The French governor of the Isle of France, M. de la Bourdonnais, of whom mention has already been made above, was a man of infinite resource, and altogether one of the most remarkable men who took part in the war. Some years before, when the rumour of a probable war in India was first spread abroad, he had impressed on the French government the importance of providing a strong fleet to protect Pondichery, in case of an English attack. This fleet had been built, and sailors to man it had been trained, by M. de la Bourdonnais, and all was ready to resist the English, when, as we have seen, the French government ordered M. de la Bourdonnais to send the fleet to France. After the disappointment of seeing the fleet, on which he had expended such pains, sail away for France, M. de la Bourdonnais set to work at once to create another. In the whole of history there is probably not a more admirable instance of energy and determination. The fleet was ready in a marvellously short time, and now M. de la Bourdonnais hastened with it to contest the rule of the seas with the English squadron.

An action took place between the two fleets in July 1746 off the coast of Negapatam, a Dutch settlement to the south of Fort St. David. The action was indecisive in itself, but it had the important effect of leaving the Coromandel Coast clear of the English fleet, which sailed away to get some repairs done to a sixty-gun ship. This sixty-gun ship proved a veritable nuisance throughout; and more than once subsequently we find it put forward as the excuse for the failure of the English fleet to be in its place or to take proper action.

The absence of the English fleet from the Coromandel Coast gave the French, now that they had a fleet of their own, the very opportunity, for which they had been waiting, to attack Madras. The English, seeing the designs of the French, sent to inform the nawáb of the fact, and to claim from him the protection he had promised to afford them in such a case. The messengers of Governor Morse found Anwár-ud-dín apparently in a state of indecision. He would give them no definite answer. His state of displeasure is said to have been partly due to the omission of a point of etiquette, which is always scrupulously observed in the East—the English had forgotten to accompany their request with the usual valuable present; but there must, no doubt, have been more tangible reasons for his refusal than this. We have seen the close alliance which the French had made with the nawáb; and it was probably no part of his plan to issue an injunction against them, at all events, until matters assumed a more serious aspect. Besides, the French had already shown, that they were by no means at the beck and call of native powers. There were reasons for not issuing an injunction against the French; there were no reasons, at all events as yet, to extend his protection to the British. But, whatever his reasons may have been, the messengers of the British governor returned without any satisfactory assurance; and the French proceeded to set about the capture of Madras.

About the fall of Madras there was never any doubt, now that it was abandoned by the fleet. The town itself was almost entirely unprotected by fortifications, and the strength of Fort St. George, which had been designed as a defence to Madras, was insignificant.

The English, as we have seen, had preferred to build Fort St. David, as a stronghold, further down the Coromandel Coast, rather than make Madras itself secure. The siege of Madras was intrusted to M. de la Bourdonnais; and both he and M. Dupleix seem to have regarded its capture as a certainty from the very first. While the siege was going on, however, Anwár-ud-dín had thought it time to interfere, and had written to Dupleix accordingly. The substance of the nawáb's letter, and the means by which Dupleix proposed to pacify him, are best related in the words of Dupleix himself. In a letter to de la Bourdonnais, dated the 21st of September (the very day on which Madras surrendered, but before the news had time to reach Pondichery), Dupleix says: "Le nabab, sans doute gagné par les offres des Anglais, vient de me dépêcher une lettre, par laquelle il me marque sa surprise de ce qui se passe à Madras, et menace, si je ne fais lever le siège, d'y envoyer son armée. Je sais à merveille ce que cela veut dire, et je crois avoir trouvé le moyen de le faire taire en lui faisant dire par l'homme que nous avons à Arcate, que lorsque nous serons maîtres de Madras, on la lui remettra, bien étendu dans l'état que nous jugerons convenable. Il faut prendre la place, et ne point écouter les propositions que l'on pourrait faire pour la rançonner. Ce serait tromper le nabab et l'engager à se joindre à nos ennemis."[1]

After the capture of Madras occurred that celebrated

[1] Quoted by Hamont, p. 50.

quarrel between Dupleix and de la Bourdonnais, on which so much has been written, and which was, until quite recently, so thoroughly misunderstood. It will not be necessary here to enter into any details of this quarrel, which arose about the manner in which the captured Madras should be treated, M. de la Bourdonnais wishing to allow the English to ransom the place, M. Dupleix vehemently opposing such a course. All the early English accounts of this period are unanimous in holding up M. de la Bourdonnais as a pattern of honour and integrity, and in assailing M. Dupleix with the most unqualified abuse. With the fuller knowledge of the period, which has since been gained from unpublished records, there can no longer be any doubt that, on this point, these early English accounts are completely in error. Full and convincing proofs of this will be found in the pages of Colonel Malleson and M. Hamont. It must suffice here to mention two facts, which give the clue to the whole mystery. Madras surrendered unconditionally. Of this there is no doubt whatever, for de la Bourdonnais himself states the fact in the plainest manner in a letter to Dupleix two days after the surrender. De la Bourdonnais had accepted a bribe of £40,000 from the English East India Company, on condition that he would undertake to make a ransom of the place possible. Of this, too, there can be no doubt; papers in the records of the East India Company are proof positive. We no longer wonder at his pertinacity.

The results of this quarrel were most important in

so far as they affected the interests of English and French in India. It caused an antagonism between the two great French leaders, both of whom were men of boundless energy and boundless ambition in the cause of French empire in India, and either of whom was infinitely more than a match for any leader, who had yet appeared on the English side. It was, moreover, eventually the cause of the departure of de la Bourdonnais from India. In its issue it deprived the English altogether of Madras, their most important town; but, on the other hand, it was the cause of that gallant defence of Fort St. David, which came like the first dawn of hope to the English. It affected the French, too, in another way not less important. For some time de la Bourdonnais remained in India, and in possession of Madras; and, meanwhile, Anwár-ud-dín began to think it was time that Madras should be given up to him, as had been agreed. There is no doubt that Dupleix fully intended to do this, but "bien étendu dans l'état que nous jugerons convenable,"—that is to say, with its fortifications razed. To give over the place, while de la Bourdonnais remained in possession of it, was of course impossible; but Anwár-ud-dín would not understand this, and surrounded the place with his army soon after the departure of de la Bourdonnais, and before Dupleix had had time to destroy the fortifications. To have destroyed the fortifications before the very eyes of Anwár-ud-dín would have been to excite his wrath in the strongest manner possible; to hand over the town, with its fortifications complete, was quite out of the question. Dupleix therefore decided to bear the brunt of Anwár-ud-dín's wrath; and the result was the celebrated victory of the French at St. Thomé, on the banks of the Adyar, of which mention has been made above.

The French had two darling projects: the acquisition of territory for themselves, and the expulsion of their rivals, the English. In the case of Madras, they had decided to sacrifice the first, in order to obtain more effectually the second. The impatience of Anwár-ud-dín was the means of their gaining both.

The battle of St. Thomé was also important in other respects. It was the first direct collision between a native and a European force, during the period of which we are writing; and it had the effect of helping to dissipate that feeling of almost awe, with which Europeans were inclined at first to regard the forces of native powers. It demonstrated, once for all, the superiority of European discipline; and the lesson taught by experience was not wasted. Mill, in his history, has a short note, which has been quoted over and over again, and which deserves to be still quoted, as it puts the whole cause of European supremacy in India in the most concise manner. He says, "The two important discoveries for conquering India were: 1st, the weakness of the native armies against European discipline; 2dly, the facility of imparting that discipline to natives in the European service. Both discoveries were made by the French." It was, in fact, the Indians themselves who conquered India, under our guidance.

When we consider that, as a rule, there have been in European armies at least five sepoys to one European soldier, we can no longer continue to hold the complacent belief, that all our victories were the result of the physical superiority of Europeans.[1]

When the treaty, which was made by de la Bourdonnais with the English at Madras, was overruled by Dupleix, several of the principal English residents, considering themselves no longer bound by their parole, escaped to Fort St. David. Among those who thus made their escape, was Clive.

The French were certain now to exert themselves to the utmost to effect a capture of Fort St. David and of Caddalor, the English town with which it was almost joined; and the little English garrison determined to hold out to the very last; for, with the fall of Fort St. David, all the English power in the south of India would fall. Four attacks in all did the French make on Fort St. David; and it was only, in one case, the arrival of an English fleet under Admiral Griffin, which threatened Pondichery and made the French hastily withdraw their troops to its assistance, in another, the skill displayed by Major Lawrence, who had then recently arrived to take command of the English forces in India, which prevented them from succeeding. The nawáb, smarting under the defeat inflicted on him by the French, had at first joined the English alliance; but afterwards, thinking their cause desperate, he left them and joined the French again.

[1] See "Expansion of England," II. iii.

After the failure of the attacks on Fort St. David, the English assumed the offensive, and laid siege to Ariancopang, which they took. This was a small place about two miles distant from Pondichery; and by its capture the French were shut up in Pondichery, which was now besieged by the English. The siege was conducted by Admiral Boscawen, who had been appointed commander-in-chief of all the English forces in India, both naval and military. It had been determined in England to strike a blow at Pondichery, which was rightly regarded as the heart of French power, and a large armament had been gathered together for this purpose, and Admiral Boscawen, who was a grand-nephew of the famous Duke of Marlborough, was chosen as the fittest person to command it. However great his powers were as a naval commander, he was by no means a first-class general. The English government without doubt were unwise in expecting to find these two qualities, in any great degree, combined in one person.

On the French side, the chief officer of Dupleix, Paradis, was now dead; and, there being no one capable of filling his place, Dupleix himself had to take the command during the siege. Though without any military training, Dupleix succeeded in baffling every attempt the English made to take Pondichery; and, at the end of five weeks, the siege was raised.

Dupleix no sooner got rid of the English, than he began to project another attack on Fort St. David on a larger scale than ever; when, in the midst of his preparations, news arrived in India that peace had been made between England and France. By the treaty of Aix-la-Chapelle, which followed the declaration of peace, a mutual restitution of prisoners and places taken in the war was enacted; and the English were once more the possessors of Madras, the French receiving, in exchange, Cape Breton.

Taken altogether, it must be said that, in this first period of the war, the French had the best of the struggle. At the very commencement of hostilities, the English omitted to take advantage of the golden opportunity given them of taking Pondichery; and we have seen for what reasons. When at last they laid siege to Pondichery, its fortifications had been completed, and it was strong enough to resist their attack. At one time during this period, we find the English entirely confined to Fort St. David; and it was only the spirit which animated its garrison which enabled it to hold out even against the French attacks hitherto, badly conducted as they had, for the most part, been. Had a really strong force, such as Dupleix was preparing, when he was interrupted by the news of the declaration of peace, with a really good general at its head, been brought against Fort St. David, there can be little doubt that it must have surrendered. That Fort St. David was far from impregnable, was shown by what happened some years later, after its fortifications had been strengthened, when it was besieged by the French troops under Lally. The English had been placed, therefore, in a most critical situation, and they owed their rescue from this to the treaty of Aix-la-Chapelle.

The articles in the treaty of Aix-la-Chapelle, which related to India, were a direct attempt to place the English and French settlers once more on the footing which they had occupied there, before the outbreak of hostilities. The home governments, and the directors of the two companies in Europe, were anxious that there should be peace in India; and they fondly hoped that the provisions of the treaty of Aix-la-Chapelle would insure peace. The war in India had naturally proved most disastrous to the traffic of the companies, and the directors were far from seeing that any compensating advantage either had been gained, or could possibly be gained, thereby. They expected now that their servants in India would settle down once more to peaceful commerce; and they were apt to think of the recent war as of a storm, the effect of which would be to clear away much of the ill-will, which had existed between the companies for years.

But there were causes which must effectually prevent any such a renewal of peaceful commerce, at all events for any considerable period. The treaty of Aix-la-Chapelle might decree peace between the English and French in India; but it could not make peace among the native powers. During the late war, the native powers had had an opportunity of learning the vast superiority of European arms and of European discipline as compared with their own; and they now quite appreciated the advantages to be gained by an alliance with one or other of the European communities. They consequently left no means untried, whereby they might attract Europeans to their side. They offered large sums of money, accession of territory, and everything else, which could possibly tempt the settlers. Even if the English and French in India had been really anxious for a lasting peace, it would, under the circumstances, have been an act of great restraint, to refuse to take any part in native affairs; and, when once they mixed in the disputes of different native princes, indirect collision with one another was certain to come sooner or later. But it does not appear that any such eager desire for peace possessed them. The late hostilities seem, on the whole, rather to have served to inflame their ambition, than to fatigue them.

The great reason, however, which rendered it so difficult for them to refuse the prizes held out as the reward of their assistance, was the great number of troops, which had been gathered together in India in the late struggle. These were far more numerous than was necessary for their safety, and were, besides, the source of no inconsiderable expense; and, as Mill characteristically remarks, "with the masters of troops, it seems to be a law of nature, whenever they possess them in a greater abundance than is necessary for defence, to employ them for the disturbance of others."

Leaving out of the question, for the moment, the important factor in the subsequent history of French and

English in India, which this great accession of troops on both sides forms; and also leaving out of the question another factor of equal importance—the prestige they had gained in the native mind, by their actions during the war—let us regard each community as placed once more upon its original footing by the treaty of Aix-la-Chapelle. Let us regard, for the moment, the accession of troops as supplying the power, and the prestige they had gained as supplying the inclination, to take part in the complicated game, which the native powers were playing. If we leave both these elements out of consideration, we shall then find both nations in the exact "*statu quo ante bellum;*" and it will conduce to a better understanding of the part taken by each in subsequent events, if we clearly bear in mind what that status precisely was.

The French, it will be remembered, had, since the time of François Martin, maintained a policy of friendly alliance with the successive nawábs of the Carnatic: the English had kept almost exclusively to themselves. The French had formed a definite plan of establishing their power in India, through the aid of such native alliance, and in this way—not by direct war, the war with the English had been within a hairbreadth of destroying their schemes at the very outset—of eventually getting rid of their rivals: the English, on the other hand, showed no anxiety for permanent possessions of any description in India. Their one wish was for commodious business places; and these, so long as they were free from undue interference, they would rather prefer than otherwise to hold as tenants, so that they might quit them, if necessary, at a moment's notice.

After the interruption, which the war had made in the course each had mapped out for itself, each returned to its own course, under circumstances changed in each case by the addition of the two factors, to which reference has been made above—strength of forces, and a consciousness of this strength, when compared with that of the surrounding native powers.

CHAPTER V.

SECOND PERIOD OF THE WAR.

Motives for interference in native affairs—French alliance with Mozaffer Jang and Chandá Sáhéb—English alliance with Násir Jang and Mohammed Alí—The French declared governors of Southern India —French power in the Dekhan—Critical position of the English—Siege of Trichinopoly—Clive and the siege of Arcot—"Dupleix-Futteh-abad"—Surrender of French force under Law—The English and French theoretically not at war—Unsuccessful French expedition against Fort St. David—Truce between English and French—The Treaty of Pondichery.

THE inducements to interfere in the concerns of native powers were too strong to be resisted by either French or English, and, as a matter of fact, such interference began almost immediately after the news of the treaty of Aix-la-Chapelle reached India. In the history of this interference, the first stage is one in which each community followed its own particular bent, without regard to direct influence on the other. The first English interference, for instance, was for the sole purpose of gaining a convenient harbour; the first French interference was for the sole purpose of placing over the súbah of the Dekhan, and its subordinate division the Carnatic, two claimants, who should be indebted for their success to French arms, and who should consequently become little more than mere puppets in the hands of French diplomacy. It was only at a later stage, when their interests clashed, that they consistently took opposite sides, under the name of auxiliaries, in every struggle. It was still later, when war broke out once more in Europe, that they threw off all disguise, and fought openly as principals.

The English were the first to act. Sahújí, of whom we have heard before, as having been driven from his throne of Tanjore, by his brother Prátab Sing, now offered the town of Dévicóttah to the English if they would assist him in the recovery of his throne. The English had for a long time eyed the splendid harbour of Dévicóttah with envy, and such an opportunity of gaining it as the present was not to be neglected. They failed, in their first expedition, to restore their claimant; and, in their second expedition, they neglected Tanjore altogether, and set to work to claim the reward by capturing Dévicóttah, without the performance of their part of the bargain. Never perhaps has every idea of justice been more completely set aside for interest. No sooner had they obtained Dévicóttah than they willingly undertook to keep Sahújí in confinement at Madras, provided that Prátab Sing would confirm them in the possession of the town they had captured.

The French had not long to wait. In June 1748 the súbahdár of the Dekhan died, and the usual struggle amongst the various claimants to the throne began. The two chief were: Mozaffer Jang, his grandson, whom he is said to have appointed to succeed him; and Násir Jang, his second son, whose claims would naturally be founded on his nearer relationship. At the time of the súbahdár's death, Mozaffer Jang was absent, while Násir Jang possessed the great advantage of being on the spot. Mozaffer Jang's first thought was of the Mahrattas, and he went to Satárá to negotiate with them, with the object of gaining their assistance in his contest with his uncle, Násir Jang. At Satárá, Mozaffer Jang met Chandá Sáhéb, who has been already mentioned as that member of the royal family of the Carnatic, who above all the others favoured the French. Chandá Sáhéb was at the present time living at Satárá as a prisoner of the Mahrattas, who, in 1741, had invaded the Carnatic and taken the town of Trichinopoly, of which he was rája. At the time when Chandá Sáhéb was made prisoner by the Mahrattas, the nawáb of the Carnatic was his father-in-law, Safder Alí, who had since been assassinated; and, at the present time, another family was ruling over the Carnatic. During his captivity at Satárá, Chandá Sáhéb had resolved, if fortune should at any future time favour him, to dispute the supremacy of the Carnatic with the ruling nawáb, Anwár-ud-dín. The present occasion therefore seemed a good opportunity, if he could only gain his release from the Mahrattas, for co-operation with Mozaffer Jang. The first idea of Mozaffer Jang had been, as we have seen, to gain the aid of the Mahrattas. This, however, was distasteful to Chandá Sáhéb; who was, naturally, not anxious to intrust the capture of the Carnatic—his great object of ambition—to his own captors. Correspondence with the French resulted in the ransom of Chandá Sáhéb from the Mahrattas by M. Dupleix, and the promise of the French to aid both himself and Mozaffer Jang. This then was the object of French interference in native affairs —to make of their own protegés a súbahdár of the Dekhan, and a nawáb of the Carnatic.

In the existent state of native affairs, the plea of right might be put forward to justify almost any interference whatever. Everything was in a state so unsettled, practice was so completely contradicted by theory and theory by practice, that it was, for the most part, quite impossible to say what was right and what was not. We must, therefore, cease to be surprised at the interference of English or French on any occasion, when their interest might be forwarded thereby. Macaulay has admirably expressed this state of affairs in the Mogul Empire of this period, in his essáy on Clive. "All rights," he says, "were in a state of utter uncertainty; and the Europeans, who took part in the disputes of the natives, confounded the confusion, by applying to Asiatic politics the public law of the West, and analogies drawn from the feudal system. If it was convenient to treat a nabob as an independent prince, there was an excellent plea for doing so. He was independent, in fact. If it was convenient to treat him as a mere deputy of the Court of Delhi, there was no difficulty; for he was so in theory. If it was convenient to consider his office as an hereditary dignity, or as a dignity held during life only, or as a dignity held only during the good pleasure of the Mogul, arguments and precedents might be found for every one of these views."

Mozaffer Jang, Chandá Sáhéb, and their French allies first set about the conquest of the Carnatic, and in one battle there fell the nawáb, Anwár-ud-dín, and his eldest son, Máphuz Khán; while the younger son, Mohammed Alí, saved himself by flight. Thus, for the present, Chandá Sáhéb was freed from all rivals; and at Arcot, soon after the battle, Mozaffer Jang proclaimed himself súbahdár of the Dekhan, and confirmed Chandá Sáhéb, as his subordinate, in the office of nawáb of the Carnatic.

On the part of the English, it serves to show, perhaps more plainly than anything else, the absence of all ulterior designs, beyond the immediate possession of a convenient commercial post, when they joined themselves as allies to a native power, that, immediately Chandá Sáhéb became nawáb of the Carnatic—although this post had been gained by the assistance of French arms—they hastened, as beseemed them as tenants, to pay their respects to him at Arcot.

But amidst all this plotting and counter-plotting, it was impossible that French and English could remain long, without coming into indirect conflict. Admiral Boscawen, before returning to Europe, saw that, with the defeat of Mohammed Alí, the younger son of Anwár-ud-dín, who had saved himself by flight, and shut himself up in Trichinopoly, the power of Chandá Sáhéb, and therefore French power, would be supreme in the Carnatic, and that the French scheme for the expulsion of the English would become an accomplished fact, and be brought about by the means they wished.

To counteract this, Admiral Boscawen strongly advised alliance with Mohammed Alí, who himself had been doing his best to obtain this; but the Council of Madras shrank from supporting a cause, which seemed so hopeless; and the Admiral returned with his fleet to Europe. This was the very event for which Chandá Sáhéb had been waiting. He left Pondichery, where he had been staying, to advance against Trichinopoly; and, had he gone straight there, there can be little doubt that he would have succeeded in capturing it. He, however, delayed on the way, having turned aside to extract money from the King of Tanjore, and this delay proved fatal; for, in the meantime, the English had learned to appreciate the extreme gravity of the situation, and had decided to assist Mohammed Alí with all their power.

So the first great opportunity to capture Trichinopoly was lost. There were many subsequent opportunities, which were lost too; and Trichinopoly, attacked again and again, never was taken. For the greater part of this period, it was the one point on which the event of the struggle depended; and Mill is certainly wrong in thinking that both sides attached too great an importance to this place. In reality, its importance could not be exaggerated; it was all-important. Its capture would necessarily have entailed the capture of Mohammed Alí, the claimant to the office of nawáb, whom the English favoured; and would have thus left the French protegé without a rival. The capture of Trichinopoly, therefore, meant nothing less than French supremacy in the Carnatic; but, as long as it continued to hold out, so long was it impossible for the French to establish this supremacy on a firm basis, so long did there exist a secure base of operation for their rivals. Both sides saw this most clearly. The difference between them was, that Dupleix, who professed to be no soldier himself, had at hand no generals who were competent to carry out his designs; while, on the other side, Saunders, the English Governor of Madras, could intrust his plans to great soldiers like Lawrence and Clive, with the certainty that they would be fully carried out.

Circumstances had, therefore, at length absolutely forced the English into alliance with a native power. Their very existence in India depended on it. Boscawen's anticipations were verified, and that at a time, when want of foresight on the part of the Madras Council deprived them of his assistance. Their alliance with Mohammed Alí was a departure, and a necessary departure, from all their previous policy. At first they had refused to take any part in native affairs; next, when the number of their forces in India enabled them to do so without inconvenience, they had, of their own free will, elected to take part in native affairs, if their commercial interests could be promoted thereby: at the stage, at which we have now arrived, they were left without any option on their part, and forced into alliance with Mohammed Alí, as an absolute necessity of the continued existence of a British community in India. So far their policy continued to be strictly defensive: they had not, as yet, like the French, any further idea of gaining for themselves empire in India.

By allying themselves with Mohammed Alí, the English had also allied themselves with Násir Jang, the claimant to the súbah of the Dekhan, with whom Mohammed Alí had not unnaturally made common cause. We have then two triple alliances: Mozaffer Jang, Chandá Sáhéb, and the French, on the one side, against Násir Jang, Mohammed Alí, and the English, on the other. The most formidable member of this latter alliance was Násir Jang. The very news of the approach of his vast army had caused a panic among the French allies. Násir Jang himself was totally given up to every species of luxury, and hated nothing more than the cares and toils of warfare; and Dupleix, well knowing this, tried by every means to come to terms with him. In this he would perhaps have succeeded, had it not been for a spirit of disaffection, which sprang up among some of the French officers on the very eve of a battle; and this, acting to demoralise the whole army, made a retreat necessary. This event had consequences more important than a mere retreat of the French contingent. Mozaffer Jang, in despair, decided to trust himself to the clemency of his uncle, Násir Jang, and surrendered himself on condition that his life should be spared, and that he should be restored to liberty. Chandá Sáhéb, on the contrary, decided to trust still in the French.

The claimant for the post of súbahdár, favoured by the English, was therefore now without a rival; and, as being the supreme lord over the whole of the Dekhan, he might be considered to have the right to nominate Mohammed Alí as nawáb of its subdivision, the Carnatic.

The recent retreat of the French had certainly inflicted considerable disaster on their plans; but Dupleix was too skilful a diplomatist to let the enemy see his weakness. He continued to keep up a correspondence about terms with Násir Jang; and his demands continued to be not less than they had previously been. The difficulty, which Násir Jang found in agreeing to the French proposals, was in reference to those which referred to Mozaffer Jang. To have restored him to liberty, and to have placed him again in his old government of Bíjapúr, would have been to renew the contest. But a few months' more warfare had the effect of making him willing to embrace almost any terms; and he had already sent to notify this fact to the French, when a counter-plot, which Dupleix had carefully laid, came to a head. This was a plot with the Patán nawábs, who commanded an important portion of forces of the súbahdár. These Patáns were brave and fierce Afghan soldiers, who, at this period, were very commonly hired to serve in armies of the Mogul Empire. The object of the present plot of Dupleix with them was to make Mozaffer Jang súbahdár. These Patán nawábs now revolted; and, in the revolt, Násir Jang was shot through the heart. Mozaffer Jang was taken from captivity, and proclaimed súbahdár in his stead. His first act was to write to Pondichery promising to take no steps without French sanction.

Thus the diplomacy of Dupleix had once more made the French party triumphant. There now remained only Mohammed Alí; and he, terrified by recent events, offered to resign his pretensions to the post of nawáb on the fulfilment of certain conditions, which seemed likely to be agreed to by the other side. To crown all, at a grand ceremony held at Pondichery, Mozaffer Jang was installed as súbahdár of the Dekhan, and Dupleix himself was appointed, by the súbahdár, governor over all the country south of the river Kistna as far as Cape Comorin, with other enormous advantages both to himself and to the Company. Dupleix, however, requested that, while he himself remained nawáb in name, the real sovereignty and emoluments of this large tract of country might belong to Chandá Sáhéb. We are quite ready to follow Colonel Malleson, when he praises Dupleix for being true to the traditional policy of France on this "tempting and trying occasion." We can also imagine the influence which such an act as the gift of a nawábship must have had on the assembled Orientals; but we cannot follow Colonel Malleson in his rhapsody about the extraordinary generosity and self-denial of Dupleix. The events of that day were the outcome of a deeply laid, and patiently elaborated, system of policy; by himself accepting the office of Governor of the South of India, Dupleix would simply, in one moment, have ruined the work of years. It is quite gratuitous to suppose, that Chandá Sáhéb would so meekly have given up the one object for which he was striving; and his force, though not enormous, was still by no means to be despised. The English, above all, would certainly have been more thoroughly aroused than ever to the necessities of the situation, and have lent all their power to aid Mohammed Alí, who, although he had made an offer of surrender on somewhat easy terms, had not as yet given in, and did not seem in any great hurry to do so. No! Dupleix was a far-seeing statesman; and it was no romantic friendship for Chandá Sáhéb, which made Dupleix give up to him the emoluments of the rule of the South of India. Chandá Sáhéb probably cared more for these emoluments than for anything else. The actual rule might apparently be his; but in reality the actual, as well as the nominal, power of nawáb was in the hands of M. Dupleix. The time had not yet come, when Dupleix considered that he could safely throw off the mask. When that time did come, we shall see that he was by no means reluctant to do so. He made, indeed, the recognition of himself as nawáb the one obstacle to a treaty with the English, by which he might still, in the course of events, have remained an enormous gainer.

The installation of the new súbahdár at Pondichery denoted the supremacy of the French. The lord of millions was really the servant of the French. The gift of the nawábship to Dupleix was nothing but a gift to the giver, for it was to Dupleix that Mozaffer Jang owed his súbah. When we reflect, that it was from the aid of French arms that Mozaffer Jang's first pretensions derived any prospect of success, that the result of a momentary distrust in the French on his part had gained for him captivity with his rival and uncle, Násir Jang, that eventually by French intrigue this rival was slain and he himself taken out of captivity to be made súbahdár once more, we cannot fail to see how completely Mozaffer Jang was in the power of the French. Dupleix was one of the most consummate masters of intrigue that ever lived, and prepared himself beforehand for every event, which the future might bring forth. Knowing every little feeling of disaffection among the followers of the súbahdár, he knew both how to repress and how to use such to his own ends. Such perfect control had the French over the súbahdár, that it is not too much to say, that any divergence on his part from the course mapped out for him by the French, would have entailed his own deposition, and the elevation of some other pretender to his throne. History perhaps cannot show a more perfect instance of the power of diplomacy. The little band of French soldiers, under the great French general, M. Bussy, which accompanied the new súbahdár to his capital, Golconda, was outnumbered by thousands of times by the forces of the súbahdár himself; but, for all that, it was the one controlling power amidst all this vast multitude. Through it French power eventually became absolute in the Dekhan, and remained so until quite a late period in the struggle between English and French, when it was given up by the French themselves. It is not the place here to follow the march of M. Bussy, who was distinctly the greatest French general in India at this period, to Golconda with the súbahdár and his forces. What concerns us chiefly, beyond the fact of the establishment of French power on such a vast scale in this part of India, is that, after Mozaffer Jang was slain in another revolt of the Patán nawábs, M. Bussy released from captivity Salábat Jang, a brother of Násir Jang, and made him súbahdár, with the usual result of a fresh and more emphatic confirmation of all the French powers and privileges.

All this time, the English held in the Carnatic only Madras, Fort St. David, and Dévicóttah; and their ally, Mohammed Alí, was on the point of surrendering to the French. He, however, kept adding one stipulation after another to the proposals for surrender: and, when these at last obtained the consent of the French, and had been ratified by the súbahdár, he changed his mind, broke off the negotiations, and determined to hold out to the last in Trichinopoly. Nothing in the history of the struggle of French and English for supremacy in India can be more important than this decision of Mohammed Alí. The extreme gravity of the situation of the English it is impossible to overrate; although the English at that time do not seem to have fully appreciated it themselves. It does not appear, as would seem to us natural, that they made any great effort to induce Mohammed Alí to hold out in Trichinopoly. Indeed, it seems that, on the contrary, all the offers came from him, and that it was some considerable time before the English could be persuaded to support him thoroughly. Perhaps it was the experience of their former alliance with him, which made them hesitate now. He had then shown himself headstrong, and unwilling to be governed by any advice. He had refused to recompense the English soldiers for the services they afforded him. He had, moreover, shown the greatest cowardice by headlong flight at the head of a large army before a mere handful of Frenchmen. In addition to these reasons, the state of his power at the present time was scarcely such as to afford much hope of ultimate success. The English may have begun to think, that, in view of such tremendous odds, inaction was perhaps after all their best policy. At length, however, they listened to Mohammed Alí, and despatched forces to aid Trichinopoly.

After some struggles, the French gained entire possession of the country around Trichinopoly, and subjected the town itself to a strict blockade, in such a manner, that it must inevitably fall in the course of time. And now comes the great achievement of Clive, which made his name famous at once and for ever—the capture and subsequent defence of Arcot. Clive saw that the only hope for Trichinopoly lay in striking a blow in the northern part of the Carnatic, and thus creating a diversion. With the consent of Saunders, the Governor of Madras, he carried this bold plan into execution, and with success. The garrison of Arcot surrendered in a panic, caused, it is said, by seeing the army of Clive calmly marching on the town through a dreadful storm of lightning and thunder. It is by no means improbable that this was actually so. With their superstition and belief in omens, Orientals are influenced by such causes to an extent almost beyond belief by less imaginative Westerns: and several instances of similar occurrences might easily be quoted. Although this diversion created by Clive met with considerable success, it failed in producing the full effect intended of drawing away the greater portion of the army, which was besieging Trichinopoly. That the ruse did not completely succeed, is due entirely to Dupleix, who saw through it. Chandá Sáhéb was eager to start off at once, with his whole army, to take vengeance on the army which had thus captured his capital; and it was with great difficulty that Dupleix dissuaded him. Nevertheless he despatched a large force, under the command of his son, Rája Sáhéb, to lay siege to Arcot. The story of this siege is perhaps the best known episode in Indian history. The gallantry of Clive's little band of English soldiers and sepoys, in successfully resisting for seven weeks the attacks of an army 10,000 strong, produced an enormous influence on the minds of the natives. It was the immediate means of inducing the Mahrattas, and the Rája of Mysore, to join the alliance of Mohammed Alí.

After the successful defence of Arcot, a continual war, between the English forces under Clive and the forces of Rája Sáhéb, went on. The English, on the whole, were decidedly victorious. The warfare of this particular period is noticeable chiefly for the attack, which was made directly on British territory. The country up to within a few miles of Fort St. David was laid waste. It was only defeat in one battle, the battle of Kávéripák, which prevented these forces, French and native, from striking a blow, which, at this time, would most likely have proved successful, at the chief settlements of the English.

Another event, worthy of mention chiefly because it has lately been misinterpreted, was the destruction by Clive of "Dupleix-Futteh-abad," "the town of the victory of Dupleix," which that statesman was raising to commemorate his triumphs. Colonel Malleson says, "Allowing for the moment his hatred of the great French statesman to stifle his more generous instincts, Clive razed the town to its foundations." But surely all, who know the enormous effect, which display of this description has on the Eastern mind, and how much Dupleix himself had accomplished by means of such display, will rather agree with Macaulay, when he says, "He was induced, we believe, to this step, not by personal or national malevolence, but by a just and profound policy. The town and its pompous name, the pillar and its vaunting inscriptions, were among the devices, by which Dupleix had laid the public mind of India under a spell. This spell it was Clive's business to break. The natives had been taught, that France was confessedly the first power in Europe, and that the English did not presume to dispute her supremacy. No measure could be more effectual for the removing of this delusion than the public and solemn demolition of the French trophies."

Great preparations had been made at Fort St. David for the relief of Trichinopoly; and the expedition, when ready, set out under Major Lawrence, with Clive as his second in command. During all this time, Law, the leader of the French forces who were engaged in the operations around Trichinopoly, had been satisfied with merely blockading the place, when a determined siege might have been successful. At all events, much time had been spent to little purpose; and now Dupleix urged Law to do his best to intercept the English force under Lawrence and Clive. This Law set about doing, at first, with an utterly inadequate force, and, afterwards, with a much larger force, when it was already too late, and the English had been able to make a practical junction with the garrison of Trichinopoly. Now, despairing of ever taking Trichinopoly, Law withdrew with his forces; and, after some battles, he was at length completely shut up in the island of Seringam, which is formed by the two rivers Cauveri and Colroon. The besieger was thus himself besieged; and no attempt on the part of the French from Pondichery availed to rescue him. Eventually Law, with the whole French force, surrendered; and, at the same time, Chandá Sáhéb too surrendered himself to the keeping of the Tanjorean general, who acted as the ally of Mohammed Alí. The Tanjorean general, after solemnly swearing to protect the life of Chandá Sáhéb, first loaded him with chains, and next, probably at the instigation of Mohammed Alí, stabbed him.

By the successful resistance of Trichinopoly, and by the successful military operations of the English and their allies, the aspect of affairs in the Carnatic was completely changed once more. The French, before the siege, had been all-powerful. Now the claimant, whose cause they had advanced, was no more; and they themselves, after suffering defeat after defeat, were at last most seriously weakened by the capture of a great portion of their army by the enemy.

The blame of all this lies with the leaders of the French forces at this time. They had not one really first-class leader except Bussy, who was at the court of the súbahdár, while the English had at least two, Lawrence and Clive. The French had at their head in India one of the most far-seeing statesmen, and one of the most skilful diplomatists, that ever lived, but he did not combine, like Clive, the qualities which make a good soldier with these. He could plan operations to every little detail required for their accomplishment; but the performance of his plans he was obliged to leave to his officers. Had there been another Bussy to conduct the siege of Trichinopoly, it must, in all probability, have fallen; at all events, after the siege had been given up, the English would never have had the chance of capturing the whole French force blocked up in the island of Seringam. It is quite conceivable that, under different management, this portion of the war might have had an entirely different termination.

The result of the siege of Trichinopoly was of the utmost importance to the English. While Trichinopoly alone remained in the hands of Mohammed Alí, their right to interfere, as his partisans, depended on it alone; but, now that the siege was raised, and its successful defence had been followed up by victory after victory; now that the nawáb favoured by the French was dead, and their own nawáb was, for the time, without a rival, they were in no want of a pretext to justify their interference in native affairs, had such been their object; and they might, moreover, have so interfered as to secure much ultimate advantage to themselves. Theoretically, they were not at war with the French; and this at least must be said for the English—that they really did their best to observe this theoretical aspect of affairs. The English troops were forbidden by the strongest commands to advance, in any case, on Pondichery itself; and this they never attempted to do, although, at times during the struggle, it was left almost without defence. The French, on the other hand, had no scruples on this point. The two nations, they argued, were practically at war with each other; and Dupleix did not scruple, as we have seen, to order Rája Sáhéb to create a diversion by ravaging English territory. After this time, moreover, he did not scruple to capture some Swiss mercenaries of the English on the seas, or to order his nephew, M. Kerjean, to attack Fort St. David itself. The English were, therefore, to a great extent hampered in their movements; while the French were unrestrained. The explanation of this is, of course, that the French considered themselves in fact lords of the Carnatic: they distinctly regarded their native allies as auxiliaries, not themselves as the auxiliaries of a native power. The English, on the contrary, always most scrupulously maintained the position of mere auxiliaries. They supported one native prince rather than another, because, as tenants under him, they imagined that they might continue their pursuits in safety; while their position under the French, or, what amounted to the same thing, under a nawáb favoured by the French, would be simply unendurable.

In referring to the state of affairs after the siege of Trichinopoly, and the surrender of Law, Orme says, that the French "would have been compelled to cease hostilities . . . had not M. Dupleix been endowed (and this at least is much to his honour) with a perseverance that even superseded his regard to his own fortune, of which he had at that time disbursed £140,000, and he continued with the same spirit to furnish more." This remarkable perseverance, the outcome of boundless ambition, to some extent perhaps personal as well as patriotic (and we cannot deny that his pure patriotism, apart entirely from any selfish interest, was very great indeed) had the effect of entirely reopening the struggle.

The allies of Mohammed Alí, in addition to the English, had been the rájas of Tanjore and Mysore, and the Mahratta general, Morari Rao. The first of these was tired of a contest, which brought little gain; and the other two were soon brought over to the allegiance of the French, partly by the intrigues of Dupleix, who promised to assist them, partly by the refusal of the English to assume an independent position, and their persistency in regarding everything by the light of the interests of Mohammed Alí. In a weak moment, Mohammed Alí had bought the assistance of the Mysoreans by promising, without the remotest intention of ever fulfilling his promise, to hand over the town of Trichinopoly to them, if it should successfully resist the siege. The Mysoreans now demanded the fulfilment of this promise; and, in this demand, they were backed up by the Mahrattas, who hoped so to manage affairs between the two, that Trichinopoly, which had, at one time, been a Mahratta possession, should again belong to them. The result was another siege, this time by the Mysoreans. Had the English taken an independent course, and carried matters with a high hand, in this dispute, the siege would have been prevented, and the war finished. The great Lawrence, among others, advised the adoption of such a course, and suggested that, while the persons of the Mysorean and Mahratta chiefs were seized, Mohammed Alí should be made to keep his word and hand over Trichinopoly. Mill puts the case with his usual clearness. "It is worthy of remark," he says, "that the delicacy of the Presidency withheld their hands from the persons of the hostile chiefs, but easily endured the violation of the engagement respecting Trichinopoly. Delicacy would have been less violated in the one instance by following the advice of Lawrence, and prudence would have been consulted by following it in both." But such a course would have been a departure from the policy, which they had hitherto followed; and, by refusing to adopt it, the English showed how far they were distant, even yet, from that position, in relation to the native powers, which the French had occupied for a long time past.

The success of the intrigues of M. Dupleix, his indefatigable exertions in raising troops with his own fortune, and the opportune arrival of troops from France, placed the French once more in a position to contest the advantages recently gained by Mohammed Alí and his allies. Added to this, a firman arrived from the present súbahdár of the Dekhan, Salábat Jang, appointing M. Dupleix himself nawáb of the Carnatic, in place of Chandá Sáhéb deceased. M. Dupleix was once more "generous," and appointed Rája Sáhéb to hold that office; but, finding him utterly worthless, he deposed him and placed in his stead, Mortiz Alí, the son-in-law of Dóst Alí—on consideration of his advancing considerable sums of money "for the good of the cause."

An expedition against Fort St. David, under Kerjean, the nephew of Dupleix, was not successful; and had the effect, for a time, of making the Mahrattas join the English alliance, and delaying the siege of Trichinopoly by the Mysoreans—a good instance of the conduct of native allies. This lasted, however, but a very short time. Very few weeks passed before the Mahrattas had changed sides once more, and the Mysoreans undertook the siege of Trichinopoly. Both sides exerted themselves to the utmost, until a truce was made, which was the prelude to the peace of January 1755.

This truce came about chiefly through the negotiations of the companies at home. For some years past, complaints had been sent by Mr. Saunders to the Directors of the East India Company in London of the policy Dupleix was pursuing. They pointed out the impossibility of a lasting peace in India so long as such a policy continued to be carried out; and negotiations on this point had taken place not only between the French and English Companies, but also between the French and English Ministers. Among the Directors of the French Company were found a good number, and eventually a majority, who were willing to listen to the complaints of the English. The French had hoped for great things from Dupleix, and, above all else, for a great accession of wealth to the Company. As long as they saw any prospect of this, they aided him; and the French Government showed its appreciation of Dupleix by making him a Marquis. They were looking, however, in their complete ignorance of the magnitude of his designs, for more speedy success. They became impatient; and at length decided to abandon all such designs, and make an effort to return to a purely commercial status, uninterrupted by any further interference in native affairs. Dupleix himself had made proposal after proposal to the English for peace, and had even offered them most important concessions; but all these proposals of Dupleix embraced the recognition of himself as nawáb of the Carnatic, and therefore the abnegation of the one point the English had been fighting for—the supremacy of Mohammed Alí.

It was decided in Europe, that commissaries should proceed to India to arrange a peace there, the terms of the peace to be ratified or altered subsequently by the authorities in Europe. Such was the state of feeling in France with respect to Dupleix, at this time, that, when the English agitated for his recall, it was agreed to without much difficulty. An agreement was however made, at the same time, that Saunders should likewise be recalled; but, for some reason or other, this last agreement was never carried out. Thus, throughout the negotiations, the English possessed the enormous advantage of having a man to act for them, who was not only cognisant of affairs in India, but ready to take advantage of every opportunity afforded him; while M. Godeheu, the representative of the French, had taken no part in recent events in India, and was besides essentially a weak man, ready to compromise everything.

A truce was made in October 1754, to last for three months. During this period, all military operations on the part of Europeans in India should cease, there should be an *ad valorem* exchange of prisoners, and deputies should meet at Pondichery to discuss the terms of a peace. These terms were agreed to on both sides in January 1755, and were provisional only, until a ratification of them should arrive from Europe. The chief terms of this peace were: that both the European nations should cease for ever from taking any part in the disputes of native powers, or from holding any native dignity; and that the possessions of both in India should be arranged on a principle of equalisation.

Much has been written about this Peace of Pondichery; but much misconception on the subject might be avoided, were it borne in mind, that, like the terms of the treaty of Aix-la-Chapelle, which related to India, it was confessedly an attempt to place the two European communities "*in statu quo ante bellum;*" and that this attempt was a deliberate one on the part of the two companies, and sanctioned by the two governments. It was an attempt to do that, which the treaty of Aix-la-Chapelle had failed to do, by its inability to entertain the question of native alliance. The struggle, which the treaty of Aix-la-Chapelle was called upon to decide, was a European struggle, and the articles in it relating to India had reference only to that relatively insignificant portion of the struggle, which had spread to India. It regarded the English and French in India in reference only to the mother countries; and had no reference to their relation with native powers, whether regarded as allies or as subject powers. It had of necessity omitted to deal with the one cause, which, while it lasted, must for ever prevent a lasting peace between the settlers—French aspirations to found an empire in India, through the medium of alliance with native powers. The remedy of this omission was the main object of the treaty of Pondichery. Its very first article deals with it. It laid down emphatically, that the two companies should "renounce for ever all Mogul dignities and governments, and should never interfere in the differences that might arise among the princes of the country." The treaty of Pondichery was an attempt to make peace by doing away once for all with what had proved the cause of war for the last six years. That the treaty, by its very nature, entailed a vastly greater sacrifice on the French than on the English, there can be no doubt whatever. It simply took away, at one blow, all that they had been striving for, the one object to the attainment of which every action of theirs had been directed. Colonel Malleson complains that by the treaty the English gained all they had fought for. Of course they did; but they had not fought for so much as the French. Nobody would dream of attempting to bring forward a particle of evidence to show, that Governor Morse or Governor Saunders ever aspired to power in the Carnatic by means of Mohammed Alí. Every act of theirs directly contradicts such a supposition. The one object for which they had fought was the supremacy of Mohammed Alí; and, now that the French had agreed to waive their own pretensions to the post of nawáb, who remained nawáb if not Mohammed Alí? Certainly not Mortiz Alí, whom Dupleix had chosen to share the "emoluments," while he himself held the actual rule.

The real grievance in the treaty was the proposal to arrange the possessions of the two communities on the principle of equality. This was quite unnecessary, and proved one of the chief means to defeat the end of the treaty. The French lost too much by this article to bear it patiently. All French governors would not be possessed with the desire to purchase peace at any price whatever, which seems to have principally ruled their commissary, M. Godeheu.

Until the ratification of this treaty came from Europe, each side was to remain "*in statu quo.*" It is to be noticed, therefore, that so far the position of the French at the court of the súbahdár remained unaltered. Had M. Bussy been suddenly withdrawn at this time, the result must have been most disastrous. The French power alone at the court of the súbahdár prevented a general conflagration.

The treaty of Pondichery, and the recall to France of M. Dupleix, who was doomed to suffer not only disappointment but insult, from the masters he had attempted to serve only too well, mark the end of the second period of our history—a period, which is in most respects by far the most important, and the most interesting of the three. It marks the almost complete success, followed by the complete discomfiture, of the designs, which the French had persistently attempted to carry out for so many years. On the other hand, it marks a distinct growth in the policy of the English.

We have already summed up various successive stages, through which this policy with relation to the native powers had already passed. The last stage of all, which was yet to come, was when, like the French, they came to look upon alliance with a native power only as a means to an end—their own political power in India.

CHAPTER VI.

THIRD PERIOD OF THE WAR.

Reasons for the failure of the Treaty of Pondichery—Events in Bengal—Destruction of French power there—Outbreak of the Seven Years' War—French armament under Count Lally—English, in the Carnatic, reduced to the possession of Madras—Attack of Colonel Forde on the Northern Circars—Colonel Eyre Coote—Defeat of French at Wandewash—Fall of Pondichery—Contrast of third with previous periods—Comparison of English and French resources in India—The chief causes of French failure due to France.

THE Treaty of Pondichery was doomed to failure; and perhaps, in the complicated circumstances of the period, it would have been impossible even for a treaty, whose terms were framed by men possessing the most complete insight into Indian politics, and influenced by the most sincere desire to be just, to have succeeded. The challenge to the contest for superiority, thrown down years before by the French, was at length being accepted in reality, and its issue was becoming more and more appreciated by the English as the days went on. Both parties in India had committed themselves so far, that it was scarcely any longer in their power to draw back; and the surrounding circumstances were such as to strongly tempt them from time to time to a renewal of the contest. A lasting peace could be made only by the home governments; and by these only if possessing certain requisites and influenced by certain desires. To enable them to dictate to their settlers in India such a peace as should be lasting, the home governments must possess, first of all, the absolute control over their subjects, so as to prevent their using to their own advantage the numberless tempting opportunities to interfere in native affairs; and secondly, each government must be influenced by the desire to promote the real welfare of its subjects by such a peace, so that the subjects of neither may feel themselves deeply wronged, and cherish the idea of winning back, at some future opportunity, by war the rights, of which they have been deprived by peace. No treaty, such as the treaty of Pondichery, by which the one side gains everything, and the other side loses everything, can ever hold for a great length of time, unless the gaining side possesses power sufficient to keep the losers in absolute subjection. In the present instance, the French commissioners, who took part in drawing up the terms of the treaty, and the French settlers, who were to be bound by the treaty, were entirely out of sympathy. The latter were filled with ambition; they were encouraged by the most remarkable success; and they were looking forward with hope to the establishment, in the not far distant future, of a mighty French power in India. Dupleix could make and unmake princes; the Carnatic was his province, over which he exercised the sway of a despot; and with the súbahdár of the Dekhan French power was complete. All this the French commissioners determined to undo. The plan was not one dictated by ignorance; it was deliberate, and part of a definitely formed policy. Let us pause for one moment to consider what this meant. It meant, first of all, that the French East India Company, as a body, considered the immediate question of silk, spices, and pepper, of such importance, that, in comparison with it, the sacrifice of the political life of their settlers in India was a mere trifle; it meant, moreover, that the French Government in Europe was bent before all things on conciliating England, and, for the sake of peace in Europe, was willing to sacrifice all that its subjects had fought and intrigued for in India. The possibility or impossibility of a lasting peace in such circumstances depends upon the answer to the question—Would the settlers be ready to suffer this sacrifice of themselves? Self-sacrifice is above the average virtue of humanity; yet, as in the case of individuals, "peradventure for a good man some would even dare to die," so, in the case of states, there have been instances, where some, rising above common patriotism, have suffered much in patience, if thereby the welfare of a mother-country might be secured. But there could be no such bond between the government of Louis XV. and the French community in India. It has been truly said that, at this period, France was disgraced at home and all the world over except in India; and there could be little in common between the constant zeal of the Indian settlers for the cause of French power, and the usual indifference, interrupted only by fits of insensate hostility towards England, of the French government. The settlers had little to be grateful for. In the moments of their greatest danger, they had actually been deprived of the sources to which they looked for succour; and now, when they may be said to have stood almost on the brink of success, the command had come from home, that they should go no farther; nay more—that they should retrace their steps. Is it a matter for wonder, that future French governors should have felt little inclined to render implicit obedience?

In framing the treaty, the English, guided by the astute Saunders, had availed themselves to the full of every concession, which their rivals could be induced to make; and it seems almost as if the English had been emboldened by their success on this occasion to make an attempt to overreach the French still further by infringing the treaty. Strangely enough the treaty of Pondichery marks the period at which the English enter on a distinct policy of aggression. The fact is however beyond dispute; and Clive, in one of his letters a very short time after this, confesses as much. The first move of the English was to join their forces to those of Mohammed Alí, in direct contravention of the treaty, for the purpose of subduing some of the minor semi-independent powers. For this they certainly put forward the pretext, that they were only assisting in the collection of rent. This was, of course, no real excuse at all. The terms of the treaty on this point were as definite as possible. The French protested against this infraction of the treaty; but, finding all their protests vain, they after a time set about violating the treaty themselves in a similar manner.

In another quarter, the designs of the English did not admit even of such an excuse as they put forward to justify the aid they gave to Mohammed Alí. They meditated an attack, with the aid of the Mahrattas, on French power in the Dekhan. This plan received the sanction of the authorities at home, and a force was sent to Bombay for the purpose of putting it into operation. The Bombay government, however, refused to entertain the project, on its own responsibility, as being a flagrant breach of the treaty of Pondichery. Advice was therefore asked of the English authorities at Madras. These had no longer any such scruples; and the English would have proceeded to make their projected attack on French power in the Dekhan, either from Bombay or from some other quarter, had not events in Bengal diverted their attention.

The súbahdár of Bengal, Suráj-ud-Dowlah, had captured the English settlement at Calcutta; and all its inhabitants, who had not been taken prisoners, had fled. The terrible incident of the Black Hole of Calcutta followed; and, to take vengeance on this, the English decided to send all their available forces into Bengal.

In the history of the growth of British power in India, the events, which now followed, are of the utmost importance. They found their consummation in the battle of Plassey, from which the origin of our Empire in India is usually dated. For our subject, however, which is strictly an account of the relations between the English and the French in India, it will be necessary only to mention the results obtained by the war in Bengal, and it will not be necessary to do more than merely indicate the means by which these results were obtained. The episode lies, for the most part, outside the actual struggle between the English and the French. It was, first of all, a struggle between the English and the ruling native power. It is true that, in the course of this struggle, the French power in Bengal, which was never of great importance, was utterly swept away; but the destruction of the French power was not the primary object of the English attack. It was little more than a means to the chief end. With regard to the difference, which the events of this war made in the relations of English and French in India to each other, the chief interest lies in the fact that after the defeat of the súbahdár, Suráj-ud-Dowlah, the English nominated and set up in his place a súbahdár of their own; and, as was inevitable, the supremacy of this súbahdár was equivalent to the supremacy of the English, just as we have seen that, in the Dekhan, the supremacy of Salábat Jang was equivalent to French supremacy. This fact is most important. It marks the stage, beyond which it will be unnecessary for us to trace the growth of English policy in India. After this time we recognise the English as having attained to that position in Bengal, which the French had gained in the

Dekhan, and from which they were to be removed by the action of the controlling powers in Europe. After having once gained the position, the English were not displaced in a similar manner. Starting from Bengal, the growth of their power, although threatened again and again, and, in some instances, retarded for a period of years, was never wholly interrupted until it had filled the whole of India. This growth began immediately after the battle of Plassey, and the progress of British power in India, during the twenty years following, was very great. We shall have to bear this fact constantly in mind, when we come to discuss an attempt made by the French to reopen the question of supremacy with the English, some twenty years after the destruction of French power in India by the capture of Pondichery in 1761.

We have seen that, in the Carnatic, English and French first came into collision directly, as representatives of the two European powers then at war in Europe; and that subsequently their struggle, though indirect, was conducted on the definite plan of opposition to each other. In Bengal their contest was more of an accident. After the recapture of Calcutta, and the defeat of Suráj-ud-Dowlah, by the English, the news reached India of the outbreak of the Seven Years' War between the French and English in Europe. This made the position of the English in Bengal a most critical one. The defeat at present inflicted on Suráj-ud-Dowlah had done little or nothing to impair his power; and the combined forces of Suráj-ud-Dowlah and of the French would certainly, at this period, prove more than sufficient to crush the English in Bengal. The English under Clive, therefore, made a peace with Suráj-ud-Dowlah; and, acknowledging his position as supreme ruler over both French and English possessions in Bengal, they tried by every means to obtain his permission to attack the French. The súbahḍár no doubt was suspicious that this attack would prove but the prelude to a renewed and more vigorous attack on himself, and, at first, definitely refused to give this permission. His subsequent answers to the same request were vague and undetermined; and at length the English, afraid of the consequences of longer delay, tortured one of these ambiguous answers into an expression of consent. They thereupon attacked the chief French settlement Chandernagor, and by its capture French power in Bengal was destroyed. Circumstances had prevented Bussy from marching from the Dekhan to its assistance. A very short time after this, at the battle of Plassey, we read of a gallant little band of Frenchmen, who had taken service with Suráj-ud-Dowlah, and who formed the only portion of that vast multitude, which did not fly in confusion before the attack of Clive. Frenchmen in Bengal might still join the súbahdár in his opposition to the English, but French power, properly so called, was no more.

To return to the Carnatic. It has been mentioned above that the treaty of Pondichery was only provisional until its terms should be ratified in Europe. It has also been mentioned that the performance of these terms would necessitate an enormous sacrifice on the part of the French community in India. In M. Godeheu, the French government and the French company had found a servant most ready to carry out to the full their policy of concession to the English. After the return of Godeheu to Europe, however, there came out to India, as French governor, M. de Leyrit, who was by no means so eager to carry on this policy. With the English openly disregarding the treaty, he determined that the sacrifice, which the treaty demanded of French interests, was impossible. The matter then stood thus. If the treaty were not ratified in Europe, war would go on again in India as a matter of course; and, if it were ratified, M. de Leyrit determined to make the flagrant breaches of the treaty on the part of the English the pretext for a declaration of war. A renewal of the war was therefore certain in any case. Only the news of the ratification or non-ratification of this injudicious treaty was waited for.

The news of the outbreak of the Seven Years' War in Europe dispelled all uncertainty; and the English and French settlers settled down to war in earnest once more. The events from this time until the capture of Pondichery by the English in 1761 form what we have called The Third Period of the Struggle. This third period is simpler in character than either of the other two; and it will be unnecessary, therefore, to follow its events with the same detail as was necessary in the first, and, still more so, in the second period of the war. During the first two periods, the English and French in

India fought, so to speak, on different levels, and much complexity was introduced into the contest by the diplomatic skill, which the French knew, and which the English did not know, how to employ. At the present time the rivals stood on an equality with each other; and, with Dupleix, the French lost that power, which had saved them at times, when destruction seemed certain, and which had, in certain instances, availed to turn their very defeats into what might almost be called victories. The third period was essentially a struggle between the two European communities undisturbed by any preponderating influence derived from native alliance on one side or the other. Throughout the period the Europeans were indeed strengthened by native allies, but these formed no important part of the struggle, and can scarcely be said to have determined its issue in any way.

With a view to striking a severe blow at England, the French Government had decided to make a tremendous effort towards driving the English out of India altogether. With this object they prepared an armament such as had never before been seen in India; and, at its head, they placed Count Lally, a brave soldier, but little fitted to conduct such an expedition, by reason of his hasty temper, and his utter ignorance of both European and native affairs in India. He went out from France, impressed more than anything else with the idea that pillaging and pilfering were universal among the servants of the French Company in India. He, therefore, took upon himself, first of all, to effect a thorough reform, in this respect, at Pondichery. This was to some extent, no doubt, necessary; but it might have been done, both at a more convenient season, and in a gentler manner. As it was, the effects of this start were seen all through the remainder of the war. Discontent and dissatisfaction gave rise to desertion of troops and sometimes to open revolt. This state of things universally prevailed and lasted until the end of the war; and there can be little doubt, that, of all the causes, which assisted to bring about the ultimate failure of Lally and his enormous force, this was the chief. In such a case, insubordination so prevalent must prove fatal. The treatment, which Lally bestowed on the natives, also provoked their hatred. He had actually plundered one of their most venerated temples, and committed the crime of crimes by blowing away six Brahmans from guns. The commissariat department of the French army, during the whole of this period, was also another frequent cause of desertion. The troops were for the greater part of the time half starved. Altogether it would seem as if this expedition were one of the most ill-organised and ill-fated on record. The English, on the contrary, suffered from no such disadvantages. The generals, to whom they had been accustomed for years, still continued to lead them, and their power continued to be reinforced by liberal supplies of troops and arms from home.

Still, with everything against him, the proceeding of Lally was, for a time, like a triumphal procession. Fort St. David fell, and province after province became the property of the French. The English were quite reduced to the possession of Madras; and, had the French succeeded in their attack on this place, English power in the Carnatic would have been a thing of the past. The English forces were, however, concentrated here; and the conduct of the siege by the French was, for various reasons, feeble.

All this time Clive remained in Bengal. The state of that province was as yet too unsettled to allow of his leaving. He, however, created a diversion by sending one of his best generals, Colonel Forde, to attack the French possessions in the Northern Circars. This diversion, in the end, proved itself a grand success. Forde made a midnight attack upon Masulipatam, which fell, and with it 3000 Frenchmen as prisoners of war. Such an event had the usual effect on the native allies. On his arrival at Pondichery, Count Lally had thought fit to withdraw Bussy from the court of the súbahdár of the Dekhan; and now the súbahdár, Salábat Jang, deserting the conquered for the victorious, came forward and made an agreement with Forde to expel the French altogether from the Dekhan, and to grant certain districts, which had been in the possession of the French, to the English.

On October 27, 1759, Colonel Eyre Coote landed at Madras with a royal regiment of infantry, and strong reinforcements of soldiers in the service of the Company. This was the force which decided the doubtful struggle. Early in the year 1760, occurred the great battle of Wandewash, in comparison with which, all the previous battles in India appear insignificant, from the fact that so great a number of Europeans on each side here met in conflict. The result was a complete English victory; and after this the end was never doubtful. Nothing short of a miracle could ever raise French power again to the position it had once held. After this, the war was carried on from point to point with success on the side of the English, until at last the French were shut up in Pondichery, which surrendered on January 16, 1761, there being at that time only provisions left for two days.

Regarded as a history of military exploit, this third period is perhaps the most interesting of all. The number of European soldiers in India was greater than it had ever been before; and the sepoys had been brought to a greater state of efficiency than ever. But, from other points of view, it is not so interesting. It is simply, like most other struggles, a contest depending almost entirely on force, and on what we may call, for want of a better term, the fortune of war; whereas the great triumphs of the struggle before this period had been brought about by other means.

On looking back at the whole course of the struggle between England and France in India, we cannot fail to remark, that, while in most respects, the powers, which the two nations could bring into the contest, were not dissimilar in point of strength, there was one weapon, which, for the greater part of the struggle, the French used with great effect, and which the English were, from the nature of the case, precluded from using at all. This was the knowledge of all the *arcana* of native politics, which brought to its possessors the power of pitting one native prince against another to their own advantage. Even had the English acquired this knowledge, the putting of it into practice could only have been brought about by a determination to gain political and territorial power for themselves, as the French had determined. Such diplomacy could in fact have no other object. As it was, the French and English, for a long time, fought from entirely different standpoints, and consequently the struggle was a most unequal one. They fought not only with entirely different objects; but this distinction of objects brought into play a most powerful weapon, on one side, which the other side could not, in the nature of things, effectively employ. The object of the French (to repeat what has been expressed more than once before) was the supremacy of themselves, brought about by taking advantage of the weakness, which was produced by native discords: the object of the English was simply their own safety, and alliance with a native power as a means to this. The object of the French was certainly the more heroic, in the usual sense of the term. It is, however, nothing less than absurd to raise them on the lofty pinnacle, which Colonel Malleson and other recent writers have prepared for them. Colonel Malleson is continually calling the attention of his readers to the preternatural dulness of some of the English governors, and takes every opportunity to hold up to scorn Governor Morse, and Governor Floyer, and the rest, who failed to profit by the brilliant example afforded them by the governors on the other side, M. Dumas and M. Dupleix. One would almost think from Colonel Malleson's works that dulness and stupidity were the inevitable characteristics of an English governor of Madras. But be it remembered that they acted in accordance with the directions of the controlling power at home, and with the advice of the members of their Council in India, and that their actions were, for the most part, strictly in accordance with the predominating opinion of the English in India. It is surely no sign of dulness (if we regard the matter from any other point of view than a soldier's, and there are other points of view from which such matters may be judged) that the English did not engage of their own free will, as did the French, in the struggle for empire. Their dulness, if such it was, did not, at any rate, prevent them from seeing that empire in India was the distinct object of the intrigues of Dupleix with native princes; and many were the complaints, which they sent home, of this man, who was doing his best, in this way, to make a lasting peace in India impossible. When the English entered on the last stage of their policy, and devoted themselves to the attainment of power in India, there were not wanting skilful governors and able warriors, who proved the equals of Dupleix, Bussy, and Lally; but it is only fair to say, that the vast empire, which these Englishmen and their successors have raised up, has been raised by precisely the means, which the French were the first to discover.

But, it might be asked, if the French in India had, during the struggle, a power of their own generally equal and sometimes superior to that possessed by the English, if, moreover, they had on their side this wonderful weapon of diplomacy, which, in its application, proved so much more powerful than mere force, what were the causes, which produced at the last their downfall and our success? It was certainly not any great excess, on the side of the English, of personal courage or military skill. Certainly we find, on the English side, great men like Lawrence, Clive, Forde, Coote, and Saunders; and their names will always be honoured by Englishmen; for, had it not been for men like these, every English settlement in India would many a time have been destroyed, and every Englishman expelled. But, much as we owe to such men, it is impossible to conceal the fact that, to a very great extent indeed, the success of the English was due to the misfortunes of the French. The foes of the French were, in very truth, those of their own household: they were the French government and the Directors of the French East India Company. After all, these were, no doubt unconsciously, our greatest allies; and to them alone the English owed their rescue from perils, from which it is impossible to imagine any other mode of escape. Was every English place on the Coromandel Coast, with the exception of Fort St. David, in the hands of the French?—the French government agreed to the terms of the treaty of Aix-la-Chapelle, which directed that a mutual restitution of all persons and places taken in the war should be made. Was French influence in India so great, that one Frenchman guided the counsels of súbahdárs and nawábs, and even influenced those of the Great Mogul himself?—the French Company, sighing because of a diminished revenue, and the French government, abjectly cringing before the wrath of England, were ready to give up all their influence, and to recall and treat with contumely the Great Governor, who had spent life and wealth for the glory of France. Against odds like these not even a Dupleix, a Bussy, or a Lally, could succeed. Such was the chief, and in all probability the sole, cause of the failure of the French in India. They had conceived a project too vast for the comprehension of either the debased government of Louis XV., or the Directors of the "Compagnie des Indes."

The most disastrous blow was therefore struck at French power at the conclusion of what we have called the second period of the war. Previous to the Treaty of Pondichery, the chances of ultimate French success were overwhelming. The grand outline was already sketched; it remained but to fill in the details. The master-mind of Dupleix had gathered together into one whole, forces previously discordant; and, in his ability to enlist all these in the cause of French power, lay an almost certain hope for the future. At a critical moment the master-mind was removed; the policy which had achieved such triumphs was abandoned; the coign of vantage was given up; and, for the future,

France must meet England on equal, if not on inferior terms.

It was inevitable that the French designs should be, in an especial manner, subject to risk, both from their nature and from their vastness; but for France it was unfortunate that a misfortune like that of the capture of Law's army and the death of Chandá Sáhéb should have resulted in their abandonment. The disaster, though severe, need not have been more than temporary. It most certainly had not proved the destruction of French hopes, as is sometimes represented. The English were still in a most perilous position. From a French point of view, the great difficulty was still the status of Mohammed Alí; and we can scarcely imagine that Dupleix would have failed to find some mode of settling this question. The whole state of India was, in fact, ripe for the exercise of that power in which he excelled; and it can scarcely be doubted that he would have taken advantage of Mahratta and Mysorean affairs to establish French power more securely than ever. The great victories of Dupleix were due to moral rather than to physical force; but it was precisely this fact that his masters at home were incapable of understanding.

The third period of the war was one, in which France possessed no advantage even in the Carnatic; and, even if Lally had proved completely victorious here, even if French power in the Dekhan had been allowed to remain and to become consolidated, the English now possessed a stronghold in Bengal, from which it would have been difficult to expel them. As time went on, the question of French or English supremacy in India was limited to an ever-decreasing area. Certainly, the Carnatic still continued to be debateable ground; but the struggle, during the third period, was one of union against division, and its result was such as might naturally have been anticipated.

CHAPTER VII.

THE SUPREMACY OF ENGLAND.

Subsequent French attempts—The "French party" in India—Privateers of the Isle of France—Way for European dominion prepared by the weakening of every formidable native state—Growth of English power—Its abuse—Hyder Alí—Confederacy of native powers—Alliance of French with Hyder—False feeling of security on the part of the English at Madras—Hyder invades the Carnatic—Critical position of the English—French forces under D'Orves, Duchemin, Suffrein, and Bussy—Peace of Versailles.

THE ruin of French power in India was, for the time, complete. In 1761, not one of the numerous possessions, which France had once held, remained; and there was not to be found in the whole of India a single native prince, whose actions continued to be controlled or directed by the counsels of French statesmen. The question of French or English supremacy was settled, and, as events proved, settled once for all. Attempts were indeed made subsequently by France and by Frenchmen to re-open the question; but none of these attempts were successful. All that the most vigorous of them can be said to have done was to retard the progress of British power.

For many years to come, the idea either of driving the English out of India altogether, or of inflicting a severe blow on England by means of her Indian possessions, continued to form a chief feature of French policy. Only one actual attack was organised and carried out by the French government, during the years 1781–1783; but, at various periods all through the remainder of the century, we find the French government establishing friendly relations with native powers hostile to England, and cautiously awaiting an opportunity to take advantage of the perplexity of English affairs. Napoleon Bonaparte, in his vast scheme, looked upon the conquest of India as an effectual means of humiliating England; but the accomplishment of such a design was frustrated by the vigorous policy carried out at the time by Lord Wellesley in India, and all chances of its success were for ever destroyed by the defeats which Napoleon himself sustained in Europe. The policy of Lord Wellesley resulted in the conquest of the kingdom of Mysore, and the death of its rája, Tippú Sáhéb, with whom Napoleon had contracted an alliance, in the last year of the eighteenth century. It is from this point that we may perhaps most fittingly date the cessation of all really dangerous designs on the part of France, as a nation, to dispute the supremacy of India with England. We do, indeed, some nine years later, find the French intriguing with Sind, Cábul, and Persia, but the danger from this source was easily averted by treaties made between these powers and the British government.

Such French designs created much uneasiness amongst the British governors in India, and the

"French party" in native states was dreaded beyond everything else. Under this term, however, was included a large number of adventurers,[1] the majority of whom were certainly Frenchmen, but who were under no direct orders from the French government, and were inspired, perhaps, quite as much by the love of adventure as by patriotism. These soldiers of fortune, who enlisted in the service of native princes, often succeeded in creating discipline and military ardour amongst forces, which, without their influence, would have been no more formidable than those described by Orme; and it is not too much to say, that they did more than the government of France to impede the progress of British power.[2] Much damage, too, was inflicted on British commerce at various times by the privateers of the Isles of France and Bourbon. Possessing a stronghold in these islands, they sallied forth to attack British merchantmen with such effect, that the number captured in the years 1793–1797 is estimated at 2266.[3] Their depredations were only put a stop to in 1810, when the islands were captured by a British force sent out for the purpose by Lord Minto.

But, however vast were the designs of France, and

[1] Some of these were Englishmen, who found themselves placed in a most awkward position, when war broke out between the states in which they served and the English. For an account of one of these, Colonel Gardner, see "Wanderings of a Pilgrim in search of the Picturesque," a most entertaining work, being the journal of a lady, Mrs. Fanny Parks, in India during the years 1822–1845.

[2] An excellent account of the most famous of these soldiers of fortune is to be found in Colonel Malleson's "Final French Struggles in India."

[3] "Final French Struggles," p. 81.

however great the injury inflicted by French soldiers of fortune and privateers, there was only one short period subsequent to the fall of Pondichery in 1761, during which the government despatched forces of any considerable extent to attack the English possessions in India. In the meantime, vast changes had taken place. Favoured by the most remarkable combination of circumstances, British power had grown with wonderful rapidity; and France no longer possessed a secure basis for military operations in India. The Treaty of Paris in 1763 gave back to France the possessions she had held in India in the year 1749, and the French were once more the owners of Pondichery, Kárikál, Chandernagor, and Mahé. These places were, however, given back with their fortifications destroyed; and, although subsequently re-fortified, they were so situated as to ensure their falling a prey to England in case of war. Such, in fact, has been their history ever since: taken almost always without difficulty, when war has broken out between the two nations, they have again become French possessions at the declaration of peace; and as such they remain to the present day. It was scarcely possible that Pondichery, situated in the territory of Mohammed Alí, could ever again become what it had been under Dupleix—the centre of a great French power. For the future, all hope for France in her opposition to England must depend on an alliance with some native state; and, in such an alliance, she will have to deal with a British power, which, even in 1761, might be regarded as at least the equal of any in India.

Almost simultaneously with the English victory in the Carnatic, the way was prepared for European dominion in India by the weakening of the most formidable native states. "Few historical coincidences," says Mr. Sidney Owen,[1] "are more remarkable than the precise synchronism of Lally's final contest with Coote, the Maratha strife with the Abdali, and Hyder's struggle with Kunde Rao." At the battle of Pánipat the Afghans inflicted on the Mahrattas a blow from which they never fully recovered; and by the contest between the adventurer, Hyder Alí, and the Mysorean general, the growth of the most formidable native power, with which England has had to struggle, was retarded for years.

Within a decade after the battle of Plassey, English rule was firmly established over Bengal, Behár, and Orissa: the province of Oudh had been conquered, but was returned to the nawáb on condition of alliance: the Emperor of Delhi himself had sought refuge with the English, and become, in reality, a dependant on their bounty. He still remained, in theory, supreme ruler over the whole of India; and the English found it convenient to uphold the validity of imperial edicts announcing to the world "that, in consideration of the attachment of the high and mighty, the noblest of exalted nobles, the chief of illustrious warriors, our faithful servants and well-wishers, worthy of our royal favours, the English Company, we have granted them as a free gift," &c. In the Carnatic, too, the English were vir-

[1] "India on the Eve of the British Conquest," p. 338.

tually the chief rulers, although, for reasons of their own, they continued to keep Mohammed Alí on the throne.

More astonishing than the growth of the Company's power is the abuse to which it was at first put by the servants of the Company, with a few notable exceptions. The history of Bengal for five years after the battle of Plassey, and of the Madras Presidency for a much longer period after the fall of Pondichery, would disgrace the annals of any nation. The majority of those to whom the direction of affairs was committed were devoid of the most elementary principles of common honesty. They had little thought for the advantage of the Company, and none at all for the honour of England. To enrich themselves at the expense of native princes was their one object. This object was best to be achieved in Bengal by setting on the throne a nawáb, who should be willing to surrender every vestige of power, and, at the same time, able to pay heavily for the privilege. Mír Jaffír had been forced to bribe until his treasury was empty; he was thereupon deposed, and Mír Kásim put in his stead. Mír Kásim showed signs of possessing a will of his own: he was therefore deposed likewise; and Mír Jaffír was once more placed on the throne, and subjected to a constant system of extortion, until, in a short time, he died worn out with grief. In the Carnatic, on the other hand, it was found more profitable to pander to the vices of Mohammed Alí—a ruler probably as worthless as any that even India has ever seen. By advancing sums of money at exorbitant rates of interest to this spendthrift, and by receiving, in lieu of payment, the rents of large tracts of land in the Carnatic, many Englishmen amassed enormous fortunes. The vices of Mohammed Alí proved a most fertile source of wealth, and were accordingly encouraged by the English, who showed themselves willing to abandon every idea of self-respect and to stop short at nothing in their subserviency. They allowed themselves—to use a phrase of Colonel Wilks—"in the exclusive character of dupes," to be led into quarrels, with which the government or Company could not possibly have any concern, and to engage in contests with native powers simply for the purpose of enabling Mohammed Alí to replenish his coffers by the plunder of his neighbours'. In a word, the Madras Council was, regarded as a body, as bad as bad could be; and consistently left undone those things which ought to have been done, and did those things which ought not to have been done. We are scarcely surprised, then, to find that in 1779, on the eve of the greatest peril through which British power in Southern India has passed, no due precautions had been taken for the safety of the Company's possessions in the Carnatic, and that Hyder Alí was able to ravage the country and burn the villages up to within a few miles of Madras, before the English were aware of danger. It was at this period, and in conjunction with Hyder Alí, that the French government made the last actual attack on British possessions in India. No time could have been more opportune for France; for, besides being itself disorganised, British power was, at this time, menaced in a greater or less degree by all the most powerful native states.

The history of India from the year 1761 up to the date of this French alliance with Hyder Alí is one of the utmost complexity. Of all the existing powers in India, no one had as yet shown itself to be without doubt superior to the others. In Bengal alone was British power so firmly established as to control, rather than to be controlled by, the circumstances of neighbouring states. The Bombay Presidency was forced to take part in the disputes of the adjacent Mahratta states, which, though nominally a confederacy, were in reality so many distinct petty powers in an almost perpetual state of dissension; while, as we have seen, the English in the Carnatic were, to a very great extent, swayed by the caprice of Mohammed Alí. To the east of the Mahratta country was the kingdom of Hyderábád—or what we have previously called the súbah of the Dekhan, considerably reduced in size by the Mahratta conquests of 1760—now ruled by Nizám Alí, who had caused his brother, Salábat Jang, to be assassinated; and in the south, bordered on the west by the Malabar coast and on the east by the Carnatic, was the kingdom of Mysore, governed by Hyder Alí, one of the most remarkable men, whether regarded as a soldier or as a statesman, that ever lived. The numerous and ever-changing combinations and divisions of these and other powers remind one of the forms in a kaleidoscope; and, in estimating the strength of the various alliances, it must not be forgotten that, at this time, European soldiers of fortune were playing an important part in the organisation of nearly every native state. For a thorough comprehension of this period, a special study of each separate division must be made in such works as Grant Duff's "History of the Mahrattas," and Colonel Wilks's "History of the Kingdom of Mysore;" but for our purpose it must suffice to sketch, in the briefest manner possible, the career of Hyder Alí in its bearing upon British power.

Hyder Alí began by showing the greatest respect for his English neighbours: he ended by hating and despising them. His policy was at first to establish and protect the kingdom of Mysore by an alliance with the English: failing to obtain this, he devoted all his energies to the formation of a confederacy of all the native powers, Hindú and Mohammedan, which should expel them from every part of India. In 1766, Mohammed Alí had induced the English to join him in an attack on Hyder; and the result of that rash and ill-considered proceeding was that Hyder, in 1769, was in a position to dictate his own terms for a peace. Bent on carrying out his favourite idea, he proposed, and the English accepted, in their own behalf—for Hyder persisted in ignoring Mohammed Alí—a defensive alliance between the two powers. Had the English faithfully observed their part of the agreement, much future evil might have been averted, and any further French attack would, in all probability, have been impossible; but, as it was, they took the first opportunity of breaking their word, when, two years later, Hyder was attacked and defeated by the Mahrattas. After this, Hyder's policy seemed to fluctuate. On the one hand, he was sceptical as to the advantage to be derived from treaties with people who had shown so little scruple in refusing to fulfil a solemn engagement; while, on the other, there is no doubt that he fully appreciated the numerous causes which would favour the English in a conflict with a native power. Some five years later, Hyder, in turn, defeated the Mahrattas, and made a proposal to them of alliance defensive and offensive against the English. He, however, paused, and once more made an offer of alliance with the English and of assistance to the Bombay Presidency, which was at this time implicated in the disputes of the Mahratta states. With the refusal of his offers, Hyder seems definitely to have made up his mind. In 1778, came the news of the outbreak of war between England and France, and he began to entertain the hope of French co-operation. He moreover brought about a confederacy with the Nizám and the majority of the Mahratta states for the avowed purpose of driving the English out of India altogether. Fortunately for British power in India, this confederacy was first weakened and eventually broken up by the skill of Warren Hastings; and, when the struggle came, it was almost confined to Hyder Alí, assisted by the French in Southern India.

Immediately on the outbreak of war with France, the English attacked and captured without difficulty all the French possessions except Mahé. This place, situated on the Malabar coast, lay in territory which

Hyder Alí regarded as his; and he accordingly warned the English that he should regard any attack as a declaration of war against himself. In spite of this warning, Mahé was captured; and Hyder prepared to invade the Carnatic with an army of more than 80,000 men and a considerable French force in his service. This vast army, which was disciplined and commanded as no native army had ever been before, began its march in June 1780, two months after Sir Thomas Rumbold, the President of Madras, had, in bidding farewell to his Council, complacently told them, "It affords me a particular satisfaction that the whole of the Carnatic and the Company's northern possessions are at present undisturbed, and in perfect tranquillity. . . . I think there is the greatest prospect that this part of India will remain quiet, especially if the Government here cautiously avoid taking any measures that may be likely to bring on troubles."[1] The Government at Madras certainly did most cautiously avoid taking any measures whether for the purpose of irritating their neighbours or of protecting the English possessions. Twice subsequently, on the 19th June and on the 17th July, when not only the general fact but many of the details of Hyder's march were known, motions urging the necessity of immediate defensive preparations were brought forward and rejected by the majority. Surely, to use the words of Professor Wilson, "The history of British India affords no similar instance of such utter want of foresight or such imbecility of purpose." When, at

[1] Quoted by Professor Wilson in a note to Mill's History.

length, the presence of Hyder within a few miles of Madras made further delay impossible, the defensive measures taken were miserably inadequate. Twenty years of wholesale corruption had produced their natural effect on the Company's finances, while luxury, and vice, and English usury, kept Mohammed Alí in a state of perpetual insolvency. Left to itself, British power in Southern India must in no long time have fallen a prey to the Mysoreans. Its salvation was due to Warren Hastings, who invested Sir Eyre Coote with dictatorial power, and sent him to the Carnatic at the head of the strongest force which could be collected in Bengal. Until the arrival of this force at the end of the year 1780, Hyder's course was one of almost unbroken success. Almost every important place in the Carnatic was in his hands, and a large detachment of the English army had been forced to surrender. For a time Madras seemed to lie at his mercy. The French inhabitants of Pondichery had seized the place, and entered into negotiations with Hyder, and were awaiting the arrival of help from France. Such was the first crisis of the war. For a time the aspect of affairs was changed by the arrival of Sir Eyre Coote. In the beginning of the year 1781, the forces of Hyder sustained more than one severe defeat; but shortly afterwards the English found themselves placed in a position even more critical than the one described above; for it must be borne in mind that the army commanded by Sir Eyre Coote practically represented the whole of the available English forces in India.

In view of the arrival of a French force, the importance of Pondichery was very great; and Sir Eyre Coote set out for the purpose of recapturing it. He was followed by Hyder, who managed to secure a strong position which effectually blocked the road to Madras. Just at this time a French squadron under the command of the Chevalier d'Orves arrived off the Coromandel Coast; and the English were thus completely hemmed in. Supplies were cut off in every direction; and Hyder, secure in his position, was far too wise to risk a battle. The surrender of the whole British army appeared to be nothing more than a matter of time; when, to the relief of the English and the amazement of all, the French squadron moved off and left the English free to obtain supplies by sea. This extraordinary move on the part of D'Orves seems absolutely inexplicable. He had no reason to fear the English fleet; for, at this time, it was far away on the other side of India. He "was not required to fight. He was required to ride at anchor in the finest season of the year, a time when storms are unknown in the Indian seas, and see an enemy starve,—and he would not."[1]

The English army, scantily supplied with provisions obtained by sea, was forced to remain inactive until Hyder at last, in July 1781, offered battle and sustained a serious defeat at Porto Novo. This is justly regarded as the decisive battle of the war. The English were rescued from a most dangerous position; and the successes which Hyder was able to gain in the future,

[1] "Final French Struggles," p. 8.

were temporary only. Twice subsequently French forces were landed in India for the purpose of assisting the Mysoreans; but in both cases they were feebly commanded, and failed to produce the effect which might have been expected from their numbers. In January 1782, a few days after a detachment of English troops had been defeated and taken prisoners by an overwhelming force commanded by Tippú Sáhéb, the son of Hyder, the celebrated French admiral, Suffrein, succeeded in landing a force numbering about 3000. The golden opportunity for French interference had, certainly, been neglected; but vigorous co-operation might yet have accomplished much. In point of numbers, the English army was insignificant as compared with the allied Mysorean and French forces; it was inadequately supplied, and on every hand there was reason to fear treachery on the part of the officers of Mohammed Alí. The French commander, Duchemin, however, from the first declined to adopt the plans suggested by Hyder, and refused to take advantage of the only opportunity for inflicting a severe defeat on the English which occurred, when Coote offered battle to the Mysoreans and French, who were together engaged in the siege of Wandewash. On this occasion Coote's army was outnumbered by at least five to one; and the fact of his offering battle at all can only be accounted for by supposing that he regarded the relief of Wandewash as of the utmost importance. After this, Hyder seems to have regarded his French allies as worse than useless. He abandoned them to their own devices, and pursued the war on his own account until his death at the end of the year 1782.

In striking contrast with the inertness of the French commander on the mainland was the energy shown by Admiral Suffrein. He lost no opportunity of attacking the English fleet under Admiral Hughes; and, although none of the contests were decisive, there can be no doubt that the general result was favourable to the French; and it is morally certain that, if Suffrein had occupied the place of D'Orves in 1781, the history of Southern India would have been changed.

One of the reasons put forward by Duchemin to excuse his inactivity was that he awaited the arrival of a French force under the renowned Bussy. This force landed at Porto Novo in March 1783, and, in the following June, was reinforced by 2300 marines and sailors from Suffrein's fleet. The conditions of the struggle were, at this time, considerably modified. Hyder was succeeded by Tippú Sáhéb, and Sir Eyre Coote by General Stuart; and both Mysoreans and English suffered by the change. The position of the French, on the other hand, seemed to be improved in every way. The number of troops they now possessed in India was considerable; and, if their object was to re-establish a French power, the substitution of Tippú for Hyder was certainly in their favour. The conduct of the latter shows that he quite appreciated the danger of invoking the assistance of Europeans, and had determined in no case to allow the French to become his masters. Tippú Sáhéb, on the contrary, possessed no such sagacity, if we may judge from what happened in after years, when he intrigued with the Republic, donned the red cap of liberty, and allowed himself to be hailed "*Citoyen Tippú!*"

Early in the year 1783, the English, now in alliance with the Mahrattas, made a vigorous attack on the western part of the kingdom of Mysore; and this had the effect of withdrawing Tippú with a large portion of his army from the Carnatic. The war in this province was therefore now, to a greater extent than before, one between English and French, influenced by the operations of their respective fleets off the coast. The main interest of this period centres in Caddalor, the port of the English settlement of Fort St. David. This place was held by the French, and besieged by the English; while Suffrein, by out-manœuvring Sir Edward Hughes, succeeded in covering it with his fleet. A French sortie on June 26 was defeated with considerable loss; but it appears to have been not only badly conducted, but also deficient in numbers. The position of General Stuart was in no way improved. His army was wasting away with sickness, he was deprived of all hope of aid from the fleet, and his plans had been, to a great extent, frustrated by the authorities at Madras, who showed themselves to be true successors of those worthies who, a few years before, had done so much to imperil British power. It is scarcely probable that a resolute and well-organised French attack could have failed; and, after the defeat of Stuart's army, there would have been little to prevent a complete French triumph over the whole of the Carnatic. But while Bussy, whose caution now presents a striking contrast to his boldness, when, more than twenty years before, he had established French power in the Dekhan, was thinking about such an attack, the news came that peace was made between England and France; and English power in Southern India was saved by the Peace of Versailles, just as it had been saved thirty-five years before by the Peace of Aix-la-Chapelle. War with Tippú still went on until the following year, when it was terminated by the disgraceful treaty of Mangalor—also the work of the Madras authorities, in direct opposition to the Governor-General, Warren Hastings—a treaty of concession to Tippú, which rendered necessary the Third Mysore War of 1790.

Thus ended the last actual attempt of France to wrest from England the supremacy of India. While the period can scarcely vie in importance with those which we have previously discussed, it affords an example, perhaps more striking than any other to be found in history, of the fact that a great power may be brought to the brink of destruction by the carelessness or ignorance of a few of its servants.